THE COMPLETE BOOK OF

ORCHID
GROWING

THE COMPLETE BOOK OF
ORCHID GROWING

PETER McKENZIE BLACK

With a contribution by Wolfgang Rysy

Second edition revised by Wilma Rittershausen

TRAFALGAR SQUARE PUBLISHING
NORTH POMFRET, VERMONT

Text © Peter McKenzie Black, 1980
Illustrations for Part 2 © BLV Verlagsgesellschaft mbH,
München, 1978, from *Orchideen* by Wolfgang Rysy,
except for photographs on pp. 50 (top left) and 62.

First published in Great Britain in 1980
by Ward Lock Limited, 8 Clifford Street
London W1X 1RB, an Egmont Company.

Second edition 1988

This edition first published in the United States
of America in 1988 by Trafalgar Square Publishing,
North Pomfret, Vermont 05053
House editor Denis Ingram
Text filmset by Servis Filmsetting Ltd, Manchester
and Hourds Typographica, Stafford
Printed and bound in Hong Kong by
South China Printing Company

ISBN: 0 943955 04 1

Contents

III Appendices

Foreword to First Edition

Orchid growing remains a popular hobby despite the rapidly increasing cost of maintaining the heating regime necessary to enable a tropical orchid not only to survive but to grow and flower in a greenhouse. Those species and hybrids requiring the warmest conditions, such as most in the *Cattleya* group, are being replaced in popularity by cymbidiums, many dendrobiums, paphiopedilums and members of the *Odontoglossum* group, all plants that can thrive in much lower average temperatures.

Orchid growing as a hobby is sustained by popular books and journals but many tend to be rather insular and specialized in their approach. This is because such books are usually written by an enthusiastic grower who tends to concentrate on the virtues of his particularly favourite orchids and the specific methods used for cultivating them; the *Complete Book of Orchid Growing* is not restricted in this way. Peter McKenzie Black is a well-known professional orchid nurseryman who has not only had a lifetime's commercial experience of a wide range of plants in southern England, but is also well aware of the preferences and techniques used by the amateur growers from all over the world who are his customers.

Most of the people growing orchids today are busy amateurs who do not employ permanent staff in their gardens. However, the daily and repetitive but very necessary chores of orchid cultivation have now been mechanized and although there is no substitute, for example, for an experienced grower with a watering-can giving each plant enough moisture according to its particular needs, such tasks as watering, damping down, ventilating, shading, feeding and controlling pests can be operated mechanically so that the orchid collection can be left unattended for several days without harm. The first part of the *Complete Book of Orchid Growing* deals very comprehensively with both the traditional and modern aspects of orchid growing.

The plants dealt with in the second part of the book are arranged according to Professor Brieger's revision of Schlechter's classification, extended by Dr Senghas. They include examples from all the groups commonly cultivated and represent species from most of the tropical countries, where they still grow naturally. It is an undisputed fact that the destruction of tropical vegetation by deforestation, pollution, drainage, flooding and urban development, coupled with over-collection of specimen plants on a commercial scale for export, has made innumerable species of orchid very rare in the wild. Nevertheless, the sad plight of many of these threatened plants is now well known and substantial conservation campaigns including necessarily restrictive trading legislation have already reduced the flow of 'jungle imports' to the temperate orchid-growing countries. There is no need to purchase these as there is such a wide range available of well-grown, nursery-propagated and disease-free species and man-bred hybrids. This book deals in detail with only a very small proportion of these popular plants but its message on cultivation can be readily applied to the great majority of orchids that would ever be encountered.

P. Francis Hunt
Secretary of Handbook Committee,
International Orchid Commission

Preface to First Edition

My aim in writing this book has been twofold: to show that cultivation, care and propagation of these plants is not impossibly difficult or prohibitively expensive and, by taking a selection of 94 species from five tribes, to show the vast variety in form, characteristics and colour there is to be found in this fascinating family of plants.

This book is divided into three sections. Part I on general horticulture comprises a short introductory chapter outlining the characteristics of the Orchidaceae and a longer chapter on the culture and care of orchids. In the latter chapter topics covered include: seed and germination; compost; containers; lighting, heating and humidity requirements; propagation; and pests and diseases.

Part II comprises the selection of orchids. These were selected from the German book *Orchideen* by W. Rysy to whom we are indebted for the excellence of the colour photographs. The criterion of choice of species was twofold: to aim at as wide a geographical spread as possible and to select those known to be commercially available to potential purchasers in the UK, Europe and the United States of America. Hence examples will be found from the two major regions: the western, covering such countries as central and tropical South America, and the West Indies, and the eastern, covering such countries as India, Africa, China, Malaya, Burma, Thailand, the Philippines and Australia.

Part III, the Appendices, comprises first a taxonomic chart of the family Orchidaceae; secondly three lists of the intergeneric hybrids of the Oncidiinae, the Vandinae and the Epidendrinae; and lastly a short glossary.

If I have helped the reader to reach a closer understanding of the orchid family, both in its vast botanical range and of its needs as individual species, in cultivation, this book will have fulfilled its function.

P. McK. B.

Preface to Second Edition

The orchid world is always the poorer when it loses a perfectionist such as Peter McKenzie Black but fortunately for us his work lives on, partly through his writings and this book. Over the years *The Complete Book of Orchid Growing* has surely given immense encouragement and sound advice to many from that ever increasing band of hobbyists who are discovering a new interest among orchids. Having had the pleasure of knowing Peter Black for many years, as did my father before me, I can vouch for his sincerity and professionalism in the field of the orchids he loved. It was therefore with much pleasure, and not a little humility, that I undertook the revision of his popular book. It is with great respect that I venture to make a few comments in the light of today's ideals in a rapidly changing world.

Chemicals, for example, have changed or been banned, and poisons used a few years ago are no longer available. More orchids are now grown as house plants indoors, including many of those mentioned in this book. The sowing of seed is mostly carried out today with the use of air-flow cabinets ensuring a continuous flow of sterile air over the work area. Meristem culture is more widespread and the need for a shaker has been eliminated. On the heating of commercial greenhouses, hot air systems and radiant heat have largely replaced the old cast iron piping which in many cases is no longer cost effective. Recommended specialized compost mixes are now far more standardized, most growers using a bark or Finnish peat based mix. I was a little alarmed at first by the recommended minimum temperatures laid down for the various orchid groups, considering them to be too low, but upon reading Section II it is apparent that these temperatures do relate to the species mentioned. If in doubt err on the warmer side and maintain a lowest temperature of 50°F (10°C), below which growth is slowed or ceases altogether.

Peter Black has described in great detail his own methods, perfected over an entire lifetime. They worked for him and they will work for others also who could do no better than to follow his sound advice.

Wilma Rittershausen

Acknowledgements

The publishers gratefully acknowledge *The Orchid Review* for granting permission to reproduce the data shown in Table 2.3 on p. 38.

The publishers are grateful to Eric Crichton for granting permission to reproduce the photographs on pp. 50 (top left) and 62.

The line drawings on pp. 15, 25 (right) and 26 are after illustrations on pp. 236, 183 and 139 respectively in *The Fertilisation of Orchids*, C. Darwin, published by John Murray, 1904; that on p. 17 is after the illustration on p. 29 in *Orchids*, A. Skelsey, published by Time-Life Books, Virginia, 1978; that on p. 18 is after the illustration on p. 25 in *Southern African Epiphytic Orchids*, J.S. Ball, published by Conservation Press, Johannesburg and London, 1978; those on pp. 19, 20 and 44 are after the illustrations on pp. 12, 11 and 19 respectively in *Orchids*, J. Oplt and J. Kaplicka, Hamlyn Publishing Group, 1970; that on p. 25 (left) is after the illustration on p. 11 in *The Biology of the Orchids*, C.H. Dodson and R.J. Gillespie, published by the Mid-America Congress, Inc. 1967; those on pp. 28 and 34 are after the illustrations on pp. 90 and 134 respectively in *Manual of Orchidaceous Plants, Vol. 1*, J. Veitch, published by James Veitch and Sons, 1887; and that on p. 32 is after the illustration on p. 28 in *The Orchid Grower's Manual* (7th edition), B.S. Williams, published by Victoria and Paradise Nurseries, Holloway, 1894.

I General Horticulture

1 Introduction

Characteristics of the family Orchidaceae

A family of plants containing over seven hundred and fifty genera and twenty thousand species, of which the flowers of ninety-four are illustrated in this book, must contain some very contrasting members of the vegetable kingdom, and from even the tiny fraction shown and described here it is difficult to reconcile some of them as belonging to the same family. *Brassia verrucosa* (p. 103) and *Masdevallia veitchiana* (p. 82) or *Restrepia guttulata* (p. 86) and *Pleurothallis sonderana* (p. 83) may each at first sight be mistaken for members of different families of plants, but all have a common denominator which places each firmly in the family Orchidaceae and no other.

The orchid flower

First, the flower of an orchid of whatever genus has three sepals, three petals (one of which is always modified) and a column. The last-named contains the reproductive organs, male and female together in most orchids (the genus *Catasetum* being an exception), the stamens and anthers, the pistil and the stigma. Thus most orchids are found to be hermaphroditic. The modified petal comes in a great variety of shapes and is usually called the lip, or labellum. It can be in the form of a slipper or shoe, an apron, a tongue and a variety of other shapes and a multitude of sizes. In the case of the brassavolas such as *Brassavola flagellaris*, (p. 64), *B. nodosa* (p. 65), and *B. digbyana*, the labellum is the largest and most dramatic feature of the flower, and these species, especially during the early days of hybridization, were used by breeders to produce, with *Cattleya*, the wonderful *Brassocattleya*; with *Laeliocattleya*, the *Brassolaeliocattleya* and with *Sophronitis*, (p. 77) *Laelia* and *Cattleya* the quadri-

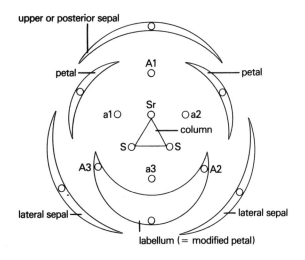

Diagrammatic cross-section of flower of an orchid. The small circles represent the spiral vessels.
S = stigma; Sr = stigma modified into the rostellum.
A1 = fertile anther of the outer whorl; A2 A3 = anthers of the same whorl combined with the lower petal forming the labellum. a2 a3 = rudimentary anthers of the inner whorl (fertile in Cypripedium) generally forming the clinandrum; a3 = third anther of the same whorl, when present, forming the front of the column.

generic hybrid named *Potinara*. The flamboyant labellum of *Brassavola digbyana*, which is four inches wide, especially was bequeathed to its progeny.

Divisions of the orchid family

The family can be divided into two main sections, the sub-family Cypripedioideae in the first, and all the others in. the second. The genera of Cypripedioideae, namely *Cypripedium, Selenipedium, Paphiopedilum* and *Phragmipedilum* are mostly terrestrial in habit whereas the other sub-families are mainly epiphytic or lithophytic and in addition these four genera have two anthers whereas the others have but one. *Cypripedium* are distributed over the temperate zones and the border between the USA and Canada, with one or two in the sub-tropics, but all the other members of the Cypripedioideae (together with the other sub-families of the Orchidaceae) are tropical.

Taking the Cypripedioideae first, and especially the tropical genera, of which by far the most numerous is *Paphiopedilum*, the most important distinction from other sub-families is in the shape of the flowers, which all have the shoe-shaped labellum or pouch which has given these flowers the common name of slipper, or lady's slipper, orchids. This pouch or labellum is in front of and conceals the lower connate sepals, of which there are two. This conjoined sepal is termed the ventral sepal. The dorsal sepal is the most prominent segment of the flower due to its great size and often brilliant colour. The petals are two, excluding the labellum, and are much narrower than the dorsal sepal and are usually at, roughly, right angles to the pouch and dorsal sepal.

The edges of the labellum are turned inwards at the base, part of the flower's mechanism to assist its fertilization by an insect, and the inner surface is partially smooth and partially covered by hairs for the same purpose.

The column is short and has two fertile anthers, one on each side of it. A third but infertile and rudimentary anther is in the shape of a shield-like plate and is called the staminode (clearly to be seen in the five illustrations of *Paphiopedilum*, pp. 48–50). The stigmatic surface is in the form of a plate at an angle to the column and is concealed by the staminode. It is smooth and polished with three indented lines radiating from the centre at an angle of 120°.

The flowers are usually single on an erect and sturdy stem, but occasionally there are several on species such as *P. lowii* and *P. parishii*. This stem arises from the centre of the base of a pair of leaves and is usually extremely hirsute.

The leaves are in pairs (distichous) and alternate and grow from a short rhizome. They are stemless and vary in shape and substance but are usually strap-like, lance-shaped or sometimes oval and pointed at the apices.

The roots of paphiopedilums are thick, covered with a white velamen and short, fibrous rootlets with which they attach themselves, especially the lithophytes, to the surface on or in which they are growing.

Divisions of the *Paphiopedilum* genus There are two main horticultural divisions of *Paphiopedilum*, those with tessellated or mottled leaves and those with plain. The flowers, while conforming to the general appearance of the genus, are markedly different in some respects, particularly in the shape and colour of the dorsal sepals, which, in those species belonging to the mottled leaved division are sometimes marked with contrasting lines running from the base upwards, as in *P. callosum* (p. 48). The cypripedes are truly the odd men out of the family if only because they have two anthers, whereas the others have one but they, the cypripedes, are more nearly akin to the primitive orchid as they have differentiated less in the process of evolution than the other sub-families of orchids. The primitive orchid, from which all the sub-families of orchids were derived, consisted of three sepals, three petals, three carpels and six stamens, the trimerous type which is arranged in threes or multiples of three; this arrangement is apparent in all orchids, although some detective work may be necessary, in which the use of the magnifying glass may appropriately need to be used. In all orchids, for instance, the labellum will be found to be three-lobed. In the description of the paphiopedilum, the two anthers were mentioned together with the staminode, the third and infertile anther, and the three lines on the stigmatic surface radiating at an angle of 120° from which it may be deduced that at one time there were three stigmatic lobes, now fused into one.

Different habits of growth of the other sub-families

Sympodial orchids The sub-families of the Orchidaceae other than the sub-family Cypripedioideae, are mostly epiphytic, but again may be divided into differing sections by reason of their different habits of growth. The genera comprising the cattleyas, laelias etc. together with the genera to which the oncidiums, odontoglossums, miltonias etc. belong have a very different way of growing from the genera to which the vandas, phalaenopses etc. belong. Both types are epiphytes, it is true, but

(a)

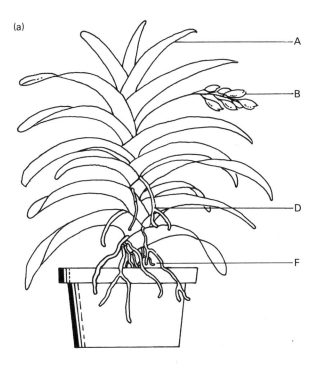

(b)

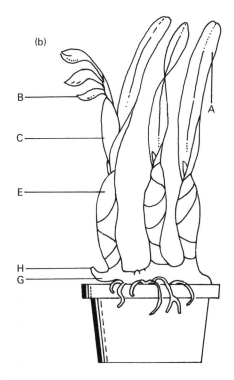

Methods of growth: (a) single stem (monopodial) and (b) multiple stem (sympodial).
A = leaves; B = buds; C = flower sheath; D = aerial roots; E = pseudobulbs; F = roots; G = rhizome; H = new growth.

the members of the former group have what is called a sympodial as against a monopodial growth. The sympodial plants have a rhizome which grows horizontally, each pseudobulb following the previous one and producing its successor from a growth or bud at its base. This growth, when immature, is horizontal for a short period turning upwards and gradually thickening to maturity into a new pseudobulb. This process is termed horticulturally, a 'bulb made up'.

The Cypripedioideae, although not epiphytes, also have a rhizome but no pseudobulbs, making their new growth from the base of the previous mature one, and therefore also have a sympodial method of growth. As in other characteristics the Cypripedioideae are the odd men out.

In the *Cattleya* genus the root system commences at the same time as the growth, usually in the spring. The roots are again of two different types, or rather have different functions. First there are roots which in artificial cultivation descend into the compost and those, the aerial or adventitious roots, which do not, but which range over the surface of the compost and on reaching the side of the pot, clamber over the rim and down the sides, and even reach out and cling to, and encircle the pot next door by means of short hairs or bristles. This un-neighbourly behaviour by the cattleya plant in captivity is its 'instinct' to attach itself to the branch of a host tree and for the rhizome to proceed along the branch, producing its pseudobulbs *en route*, covering it with foliage and blossoms, at the same time as the roots perform their function of anchors. It has literally been the downfall of many orchid plants of the cattleya alliance, and of other orchids, firstly to be so easily detected and then to be collected by man, the great predator, by the simple if expedient method of chopping down the tree.

The roots of the cattleya are thick and fleshy and are white with a green 'growing tip', of about 1.5 cm ($\frac{1}{2}$ in). A transverse section shows the white part to be a thick sheath, which is called the velamen and which surrounds and protects the interior and vulnerable cells of the roots. The green growing tip, together with the foliage is the means whereby the plant derives nourishment by the process of photosynthesis. It has been found that if an aerial root needs to be cut, i.e. when the plant is moved from its encircled neighbour, it usually branches at the cut. The velamen consists of large cells forming a spongy tissue which absorbs nutrients through the moist air.

In addition to forming the new growths at their bases, the pseudobulbs of the odontoglossums, the lycastes, the cymbidiums and many more, start their inflorescences there. In the cymbidiums the vegetative growth often appears at the same time as the flower bud and it is sometimes difficult to differentiate between them. Most of the dendrobiums, although sympodial in growth, have much more slender pseudobulbs than those of the previously named orchids and the dendrobiums are cylindrical and much closer together on the rhizome.

The site of initiation of the inflorescence varies greatly between the different genera. In the odontoglossums, oncidiums, miltonias, lycastes and cymbidiums and many others the flower spike rises from the base of the pseudobulb, but in the cattleya it emerges, in the case of the bifoliates, from between the pair of leaves at the top of the pseudobulb, and in the labiates at the junction between the single leaf and the pseudobulb. The slender, cylindrical stems of the dendrobiums have nodes at regular intervals along their entire length and the inflorescences appear from these, some-times in solitary flowers and sometimes in clusters. These nodes also are the point where the leaves and roots emerge. In paphiopedilums the flower bud arises from the centre of a pair of opposite leaves.

Monopodial orchids The monopodial method of growth is quite distinct from the sympodial in that there is not a rhizome but a single stem which continues its growth from its apex. Typical of plants having this kind of growth are *Vanda* and its allies. These genera are distributed over the Far East. There are two kinds of vanda, the strap-leaved and the terete, and many hybrids have been made, particularly in Singapore and Hawaii, between these two types. The resultant hybrid between a terete and a strap-leaved vanda is called a semi-terete.

The leaves, roots and the inflorescence arise from nodes along the entire length of the stem in the case of the terete vandas, and the inflorescences at the axil of the leaf, in a similar manner to those of the dendrobiums. The terete vandas are really climbing plants and the roots are fleshy and silvery when dry, green when moist. The velamen has a similar function to that in cattleyas and consists of a ring of dead cells which are spongy, and absorb nutriments from the air. The roots with their hairs enable the plant to climb towards the light, which is why the flowers are toward the upper part of the stem. The strap-leaved vandas, although the shape of the flowers is similar to that of the terete, are altogether shorter and are not given to climbing.

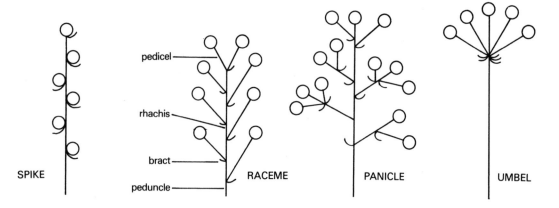

Types of inflorescence. The spike has sessile flowers; the raceme has stalked flowers; the panicle is a branched raceme; and in the umbel the flower stalks emanate from the same point.

Table 1.1 Characteristics of some of the Orchidaceae

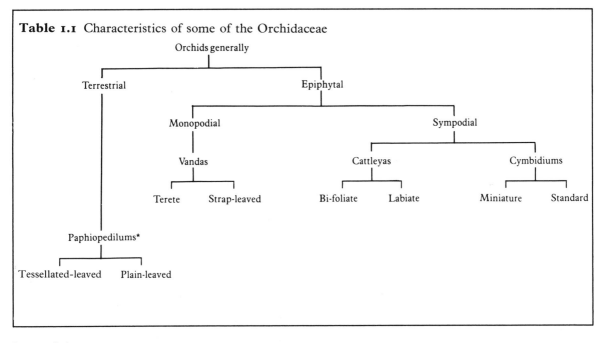

*see text below

Vanda coerulea sends out its roots in the typical manner of vandas but these do not all attach themselves to the branches of trees and therefore perform only the function of deriving nourishment from the air. All these characteristics may be confusing to the layman but they are of essential value to the taxonomist.

The main stem of vandas can often send out branches from the nodes which are in every way similar to it, and have leaves and flowers and roots identical with those on the main stem.

Chief characteristics of the Orchidaceae

The family can be divided horticulturally into two groups—the terrestrial and the epiphytal. The main terrestrial tropical kinds are members of *Paphiopedilum*, of which there are two sorts, the tesselated-leaved and the plain-leaved. The epiphytes can be divided into two groups, the sympodial and the monopodial, but the *Cypripedioideae* although not epiphytic but terrestrial, have a sympodial method of growth. The monopodial are mostly vandaceous (see Appendix). Vandas proper can be put into two further divisions, those

with terete leaves and those with strap leaves. The sympodial orchids are the cattleyas, the oncidiums, the lycastes etc. (See Appendix for a breakdown of the Oncidiinae.) Cattleyas proper

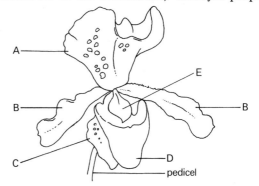

The flower of a terrestrial orchid – *Paphiopedilum*.
A = dorsal sepal; B = petals; C = lateral sepals conjoined to form synsepalum; D = labellum; E = Staminode.

are again in two groups, the bi-foliate and the labiate and cymbidiums divide into miniature and standard.

There are undoubtedly further horticultural divisions which can be thought up but the above is a simple chart for the benefit of the non-botanist.

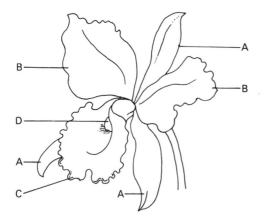

The flower of an epiphytic orchid – *Cattleya.*
A = sepal; B = petal; C = labellum; D = column.

Summary of main characteristics

1 All orchids have three sepals, three petals and a column.

2 The column contains the reproductive organs.

3 The anthers in the column are suppressed to two in the Cypripedioideae and one in all others.

4 The pollen in the anthers is coherent, granular or waxy.

5 The third petal is modified sometimes into eccentric forms.

6 The ovary is inferior (i.e. below the rest of the flower).

Habitat in the wild of terrestrial and epiphytic orchids

Tropical orchids are distributed over a quarter of the land surface of the entire earth, but half the land surface of the tropics to which they are confined is unsuitable for epiphytes as it contains deserts, semi-deserts, the tops of the higher mountain ranges where the temperatures are too low, the bare and treeless regions and pockets which, due to local causes, do not receive their quota of tropical rain or receive them in such diminished quantity that orchids cannot exist.

The tropical climate depends upon the sun's position relative to the earth. When the sun is south of the equator, the air beneath it is heated and rises and the winds and currents of air flow in from the north and north-east to replace it. At first they are comparatively dry as they pass over a large proportion of land in the northern hemisphere, but they progressively become charged with moisture. In the same way, when the sun is proceeding northwards of the equator the reverse phenomenon occurs, i.e. the winds are from the south but due to the greater area of ocean surface in the southern hemisphere over which the winds pass, they are more charged with moisture. This accounts for most places within the tropics, allowing for local orographic influences, having a wet and dry season, and for the equatorial region having least variations in temperature and rainfall.

The orchids dealt with here are to be found in two different regions, if these vast territories can be termed such, confined within the tropics and sub-tropics. The first, the western, includes Central and tropical South America together with the West Indies. The second, the eastern, which is more widely dispersed, embraces India, Africa, China, Taiwan, Burma, Thailand, the former Indo-China, the Philippines, the East Indies and Australia, especially the York Peninsula in Northern Australia.

All orchids need moisture and humidity in order to grow and to propagate themselves, some more than others. The different needs for moisture and humidity express themselves by different orchids being found, on the one hand, in tropical swamps and low-lying rain forests and, on the other, in the Andes and Cordilleras of South America and on mountains such as Kinabalu in North Borneo. As well as moisture, tropical orchids require warmth, and again the demands for this vary vastly. The genera growing at low levels in river valleys and swamps near the Equator receive intense heat from the sun at all times of the year while those on the higher ground of the lower slopes of mountains have the same number of hours of heat but of a lesser degree of intensity. This lower temperature of the mountains itself varies from the near freezing at dawn to the higher at noon (higher than at low levels) and it must be remembered that the sun in the tropics is overhead at noon and has a drying-out effect on the vegetation growing on the mountains. The climatic conditions in the equatorial belt are fairly constant annually, but the diurnal temperatures can vary greatly i.e. from, say, 35°C

(95°F) by day to as little as 21°C (70°F) at night.

Both the swamp-dwelling orchids and the mountaineers require a fall in the night temperature in order to function properly by means of photosynthesis, the plants making their growth during the hours of darkness.

The trees which have their habitats in the rain forests are broad-leaved and evergreen because the temperature and rainfall are favourable for continuous growth throughout the year. Due to the well distributed rainfall the earth is constantly wet, which has two effects—it enables the trees to continue their growth through their roots, never deprived of nourishment, and it also makes for a high humidity which stimulates the germination and growth of orchids.

The orchids and other epiphytes which have their habitats in the mountainous regions grow and thrive at altitudes of 600 m (2000 ft) to upwards of 3000 m (10000 ft). Instead of having constant rain they have had to adapt themselves in some cases to a dry season. This is brought about by the sun which moves from the Equator to the Tropic of Cancer, back to the Equator and on to the Tropic of Capricorn, leading the belt of trade winds which bring rain or a dry period depending on whether they blow from the ocean, as they do on the east coast of South America, or off-shore as they do on the west coast. The influence of these mountainous regions has an effect on the climate of the terrain on both sides either causing precipitation and in consequence much rain, or depriving the adjacent countries and making them arid and not suitable for orchids.

Different habitats in the Philippines

It will be instructive to take a region in the eastern hemisphere which lies between 5° and 20° north of the equator, and which is the habitat of a great range of orchids, particularly dendrobiums, phalaenopses and vandas and many others. From its latitudes the Philippines have intense tropical sunlight and there are no less than four main types of climate.

1. The areas which have a definite wet and dry season, wet during the summer which is from June to November and dry in the winter and spring, from December to April, and which include the western side of northern and central Luzon and the western portions of Mindanao, Panay, Negros and Palawan.

2. The region having rain the year round with an intensification in the winter, and no dry season. This includes the east coast of south Luzon, Samar, eastern Leyte and the eastern mountains of Mindanao.

3. The region having continuous rain as in (2), also with no dry season but with no intensification of rainfall. This is eastern Mindoro, the western coast of Luzon and the western region of Leyte, the island of Bohol and west central Mindanao.

4. The zone which has a dry season of one to three months, with no period of maximum precipitation and which includes the east central part of Luzon, the eastern parts of Panay and Legros and part of northern and western Mindanao.

To analyse these types of climate roughly, reveals several interesting facts which confirm the influence of mountainous country on the regions to either side. Firstly there is an abundance of rain, even in those zones which have a dry period of from one to six months; with the rain there is high humidity of 95.8° down to 68.3° as in Manila which has a dry season of six months. The average rainfall in Manila is 204 cm (82.07 in), which contrasts with Baguio, in typhoon and cyclone country, which has an annual average rainfall of 442 cm (176.57 in), the wettest month being August, which receives no less than 112 cm (44.79 in).

Average figures for temperature, especially annual figures, are misleading, however, and Baguio, in addition to being one of the main centres for orchids, and orchid collecting, is much favoured by having an equable climate in the summer months; the temperature seldom rises above 22.8°C (73°F) or goes below 13.5°C (56°F). It is sited on a plateau at 1500 m (5000 ft) elevation and is only 80 km (50 miles) from Manila and so is much in evidence as a relief from the rigours of the hot season there.

The forests in which the orchids have their habitat are of two different kinds; the lower one clothes the slopes up to Baguio, containing the tall, resinous dipterocarp trees with their rough coarse bark which act as host to dendrobiums, phalaenopses, erias, renantheras and many other epiphytes. The higher forest consists of dwarf trees covered with mosses, lichens and ferns and, of course, orchids such as bulbophyllums, oberonias, dendrochilums and the blue *Dendrobium victoria-reginae* (which has been found to be difficult to cultivate in Manila because of its long dry season).

The lower forest is, at least on the slopes up to 900 m (3000 ft), hot, steamy and almost airless. The orchids grow at the top of the trees, 45 m (150 ft) high, in their struggle for light. In the higher forest it is difficult to penetrate the luxuriant undergrowth and there the orchids grow on the low trees and bushes in the continuous rain and fog with low cloud adding to the humidity.

Other orchid habitats

Some of the habitats of different genera have been briefly described in the preceding paragraphs. There are many more, some of which are so bizarre as to be incredible, but surely the most strange is an orchid *Rhizanthella gardneri* discovered in 1928 by a farmer in Western Australia who turned it up while ploughing. It grows and flowers entirely underground. It has since (1978) been found by an Australian botanist, and by another farmer.

One of the oddest discoveries was that of *Paphiopedilum druryi*, found on the Travancore Hills in the southernmost part of India. It is odd because there are no other *Paphiopedilum* species within hundreds of miles of its habitat.

The different habitats of *Paphiopedilum concolor* (p. 49) show how a species may be found in one area and again in a quite different one. It was first discovered in 1859 near Moulmein in Burma, growing in hollows in the rock which were filled with humus, by the eponymous Rev. Parish, and at about the same time in several different though similar places. However, fifty years or so later it was found near Champon, in the Birds' Nests Islands growing on limestone cliffs facing the sea.

The habitat of *Cattleya bowringiana* is on the cliffs at the edge of a torrent flowing over a succession of waterfalls. It is a native of British Honduras and Guatemala and the dry season is counteracted by the rapid evaporation of the mist from the waterfalls whereas the continuous rainfall at other times of the year ensures that the atmosphere is always highly humid. This habitat is similar to that of *Disa uniflora*, a terrestrial orchid from Cape Province in South Africa, except for the temperature. The disa has its home on Table Mountain where conditions are cool but moist.

Odontoglossum grande (p. 108) was discovered in 1839 by Ure-Skinner in dark ravines near the city of Guatemala. It is thus assured of constant shade and moisture. The temperature range is between 15.5°C (60°F) and 21°C (70°F). This habitat is very different from that of *O. crispum*, living on the western branches of the eastern Cordillera. Bogota is the centre of its territory which is 288 km (150 miles) long. It grows at an altitude of 2250–2640 m (7500–8800 ft) in openings in forests mainly consisting of cinchona trees, walnuts and evergreen oaks on the branches of which it makes its home, sometimes in partial shade, and sometimes in full sun but never in the deepest gloom of the primaeval forest.

Epidendrum variegatum var. *coriaceum* from South America and the West Indies is found growing on fallen logs exposed to the full sun.

Habitats of African orchids   *Aërangis kotschyana* favours lower altitudes and higher temperatures and grows on old cypress trees in the Zambesi valley and in the Amatongas valley in Mozambique.

Aërangis mystacidii grows at an altitude of 900–1200 m (3000–4000 ft) clinging to small branches in deep shade.

Aërangis verdickii must have adequate humidity and grows on the outer branches of rough-barked trees in Rhodesia (Zimbabwe).

Aëranthes africana, which was discovered in 1974 south-east of Salisbury, grows on east-facing ridges 1500 m (5000 ft) high. It favours *Podocarpus* trees where mature plants resemble tree shoots in shape, size and colour.

Two mystacidiums have very different habitats. *M. gracile* found in eastern and southern Africa and east of Salisbury, flourishes at high altitudes where it has continuous mist with cool days while *M. capense* grows in hot, dry conditions in dry acacia savannah in East Cape Province.

Restrepias grow at an altitude of 2100–3600 m (7000–12000 ft) on the moss covering the trunks of trees in a very humid atmosphere among the mountains of tropical America. This humidity, however, is misleading for at the great altitude of 3600 m (12 000 ft) the air is capable of containing only about a quarter of the moisture of that at sea level, due to the reduction in atmospheric pressure at that altitude.

2 Culture and care

Seed and germination

Orchid seed is relatively minute and too tiny to be distinguished, one particle from the other. It is just like fine powder, with notable exceptions such as that of the paphiopedilums which is larger, harder and clearly recognisable as seed. Most orchid seed is pale greenish-white in colour, the green being the nucleus; an exception is paphiopedilum seed which is dark brown. Under a low powered microscope the seed of paphiopedilums is like a fat banana in shape, but there are thinner particles of chaff which have no nucleus and are not viable. The seed of other genera such as that of the cattleyas and allied genera, seen under the microscope, shows the nucleus clearly as a green shadow, but there are usually other particles of distorted shapes and smaller size which contain no nucleus and which are not viable. The seed of miltonias is a fine golden yellow and there is less chaff than in other genera. The lightness of the seed is an indication that it is designed to be wind-borne; this is particularly true of the seed of nearly all the epiphytes. When the capsule dehisces the seed is carried by the wind to settle, some on 'stony ground', where it does not have a chance to germinate, and some in the crotch of a tree or in the interstices of rough bark. There is enough humus in these locations to enable the tiny seed to germinate, but this depends upon a number of other factors, such as predators, exposure to sun, or not enough exposure to sun but to rain and wind; and even when germination has taken place and the plant is sizeable, it is vulnerable to the depredations of slugs and snails and all the other predators which inhabit the tropical jungle.

The seed capsule contains a varying number of seed but is truly remarkable in that some species have upwards of two million viable seed. It is perhaps fortunate that only a very small proportion does germinate and grow into adult plants. Charles Darwin estimated what would happen if all the seed in a single plant of the English *Dactylorhiza maculata* grew into mature flowering plants. *Dactylorhiza maculata* bears above 30 capsules, each containing about 6200 seed, in total 186 300 plants. An acre of land would hold 174 240 plants, 30 cm (1 ft) apart allowing for 400 bad seed in each capsule. 'At the same rate of increase the grandchildren would cover a space slightly exceeding the island of Anglesey; and the great grandchildren of a single plant would nearly clothe (in the ratio of 47:50) with one uniform green carpet the entire surface of the land throughout the globe. But the number of seeds produced by one of our common British orchids is as nothing compared to that of the exotic kinds.'

Pollination by insects

Most orchid flowers are pollinated by insects, some by various kinds of bee and fly and some at night by moths. *Angraecum sesquipedale* (p. 124) is one of those fertilized by a moth. This Madagascan species has a spur-like nectary, 30 cm (12 in) long, below the labellum, and only an insect with a proboscis equally long is capable of pollinating the flower. It was 40 years after Darwin had postulated the existence of such an insect and the process by which the flower was fertilized that his idea was verified by the discovery of just such an insect, a moth, much to the discomfiture of those entomologists who had scoffed at his theory.

In the cattleyas with their flamboyant labellums, the flower is pollinated by a large insect such as a bee which, attracted by the perfume and the honey guides (those lines of contrasting colour leading to the throat of the labellum), lands on the labellum, forces its way towards the nectar and in so doing depresses the labellum and takes its fill of the nectar. In withdrawing the insect backs out, there being insufficient room to turn round, and in so

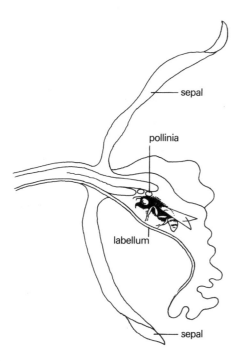

Pollination of cattleya flower by bee. Bee depresses the labellum on entering and removes one or more of the pollinia on retreating backwards.

doing removes the pollinia which lodge on its head. The pollinia are placed below the apex of the column by nature for this purpose. On visiting another cattleya flower the bee repeats the routine but this time, on backing out, the pollinia are deposited in the stigmatic cavity, thus completing the first part of fertilization. The stigmatic cavity is located just below the apex of the column and behind the pollinia, which are again removed when the bee backs out.

Spring-like mechanism in Catasetum

Perhaps the genus *Catasetum* has the most ingenious method of ensuring pollination. There are two sections in the genus, one of which has perfect flowers, i.e. male and female reproductive organs in the same flower (or hermaphroditic flowers like most other orchids) and the other, the *Orthocatasetum*, has male flowers and female flowers, often on the same plant, and very rarely hermaphroditic flowers. A bee settles on the labellum of a male flower on which there is no nectar but part of

the labellum has an enticing taste (to a bee) and so he gnaws it. There are two very sensitive antennae with their ends projecting and the bee touches one of these (in *C. saccatum*, the left one) and the pollen is ejected by means of a spring-like pedicel attached to the pollinia. It strikes the bee with considerable force and becomes attached to the thorax because it is sticky. On visiting another flower, a female, the pollen is removed and the female flower is fertilized.

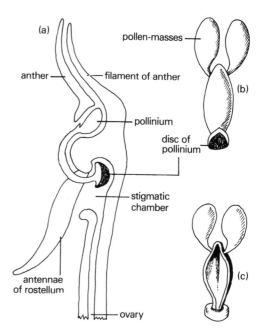

Catasetum saccatum: flower structure. (a) Diagrammatic section through the column with all the parts a little separated. (b) Pollinium, upper surface. (c) Pollinium, lower surface, which before removal lies in close contact with the rostellum.

Fertilization of Paphiopedilum

The fertilization of paphiopedilums is slightly different from the other various methods by which the continuance of the race is ensured. In the case of *Paphiopedilum callosum* (p. 48) an insect attracted by the alluring smell (there is no nectary in *P. callosum* but the base of the labellum must be tasty to a bee) enters the labellum, which is slipper-shaped, at its widest aperture which is just in front of the disc-like organ clearly shown in the illustration (the staminode), and commences to gnaw at the hairs at the bottom of the column. When he has absorbed all that he wants, or arrives at less tasty hairs, he looks for a way of escape, which is by one of two routes, one on each side of the staminode, and in passing through one of these narrow gaps, he removes the pollen on that side. It must be remembered that there are two anthers in the genus *Paphiopedilum* one on each side of the staminode. The stigmatic surface is in the form of a disc, and is behind the staminode at an angle to it. The surface is not viscid but polished and with a depression like three lines radiating from the centre at an angle of 120°. When the bee visits another flower he deposits the pollen, which is sticky and easily adheres to the centre of the depression. It must be noted that in many cases the paphiopedilums, with their trap-like pouch or labellum propagate themselves vegetatively, rather than by the agency of insects, for a bee a little larger than the apertures can enter but finds it impossible to escape and will die of starvation. The plants, therefore, propagate themselves by the new growths they make and by the spreading of their roots into the surrounding ground. Man, however, is better able to effect the cross-fertilization of this genus by removing the pollen by means of a pointed instrument, such as a tooth-pick, and placing it on the stigmatic surface of another and different flower.

Fertilization of Dendrobium

In the case of *Dendrobium*, such as *Dendrobium nobile* (p. 61), the task, for an insect, is much simpler and less hazardous. It will perhaps be interesting to see what happens after the dendrobium flower has been fertilized, either by an insect or by man in a greenhouse. After fertilization, and after a period of two days, the perianth (sepals and petals) fades and the upper part of the column starts to thicken and to become hemispherical in shape. Then after a further period of about three weeks, the pollen tubes begin to penetrate the ovary (which is just beneath the flower and appears to be part of the flower stem) in six strong bundles and to place themselves one on each side of the three placentas. After a further three weeks, during which time the ovary together with the placentas have thickened and lengthened, these divide into two ridges each of which produces

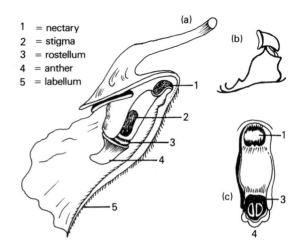

1 = nectary
2 = stigma
3 = rostellum
4 = anther
5 = labellum

Dendrobium species: flower structure. (a) Lateral view of flower with the anther in its proper position before the ejection of the pollinia. All the sepals and petals have been removed except the labellum which is longitudinally bisected. (b) Outline of column viewed laterally after the anther has ejected the pollinia. (c) Front view of column showing the empty cells of the anther after it has ejected the pollinia.

numerous minute papillae (small, fleshy projections) but there are, as yet, no ovules. After two more months, however, the placentas are covered with numerous ovules with the pollen tubes still lying on each side of each placenta. After a further month or so, the ovules are fully developed and the ovary has reached its full size. After roughly four months from pollination, the pollen tubes have entered the micropyle (a minute orifice in the ovule through which the pollen tube passes to fertilize the nucleus) and the process is nearing its end. A further fortnight sees the remaining pollen tubes complete their function and the ovary or, by now, the capsule will need only a further two or three weeks to ripen. The preceding facts refer to fertilization in a glasshouse after the pollen has been transferred by the agency of man (instead of a bee) and it must be considerably more rapid in nature.

The process of fertilization and germination varies considerably with different genera and species. *Phaius grandifolius* requires much less time to complete fructification and the process has finished in two months, and *Paphiopedilum insigne* in four months; the speediest are some of the hardy terrestrial orchids which are pollinated and germinate in eight or nine days to a fortnight.

There are very few orchids which are capable of self-fertilization, among them being *Disa crassicornis* from South Africa, the pendulous and deciduous *Dendrobium cretaceum* from India and Burma and two North American species *Gymnadenia tridentata* and *Platanthera hyperborea*.

Pollination by man

The procedure by which man pollinates an orchid is mechanically identical to that by which an insect pollinates it, except that man has advantages. For instance, he can operate at any time of day or night, he has the pod parent and the pollen parent together on a bench; the operation is not haphazard and is the result of quite a different quest from that of an insect searching for nectar with no intention of fertilizing a beautiful orchid.

The implement most often used by a hybridizer when pollinating is a tooth pick or a matchstick with a point sharpened into a chisel shape. Some genera are easier to pollinate than others; among the easier ones are the cattleyas and the cymbidiums, and among the more difficult are the paphiopedilums.

As an example, the cattleya is taken first. The two potential parent plants are arranged together on a bench in the greenhouse, as no laboratory precautions as regards sterility are necessary at this stage. A sheet of clean paper is placed under them in case the pollinia are dropped, so that they can be found easily. A note book is needed to enter the names of the parents, the date, etc. Two matchsticks with chisel points are used, and the pollinia are removed from the first plant with a matchstick, and placed on the paper still attached to the matchstick. The pollinia are beneath the anther cap which is hinged and easily removed and usually the pollinia come away with the anther cap. The pollinia are in two pairs (in *Laelia*, four pairs) and are yellow and disc-like. The pollinia of the second flower are then detached in the same way. One pollen mass or disc is then placed, still at the end of its matchstick, on to the stigmatic surface of a flower. The other 'pollinated' matchstick is used in the same way with the other flower. The stigmatic surface is a depression just behind the site of the pollen cap. The result is that each flower has been fertilized by the other one and six pollen discs are left over to be used in pollinating other flowers if desirable. The paphiopedilum is difficult because the pollinia are in an awkward place behind the staminode and the stigmatic surface; the plate at an angle to the column with three lines radiating from it at an angle of 120° is even more inaccessible. One way out of the dilemma of how to reach the stigmatic plate with the pollen, is to cut off the labellum at its base, but a better way is to employ a sharp safety razor blade and excise a little portion of the sole of the slipper, thus revealing the stigmatic surface. The matchstick is used again to remove the pollinia; the flower to be fertilized is placed horizontally on the bench, with the pot wedged on each side, and the pollen is placed in the middle of the stigmatic plate where the lines converge.

The cymbidium is pollinated in a similar manner to the cattleya as are the miltonia, the odontoglossum and many other epiphytal orchids.

After a period of months (see the section regarding *Dendrobium nobile* in this chapter) which varies with the different genera, the pod is mature and the seed ready to be sown. If it has partially dehisced it is removed from the plant with a sharp knife and placed on clean paper for several days to allow the dehiscing to continue. The seed pod is then tapped gently to empty the pod, and the paper is then folded until sowing time. The pod must be kept in a cool dry atmosphere; the humid conditions in a greenhouse are likely to cause fungus or mould infections and the seed rendered useless.

Sowing the seed

Before the seed which has been kept in the paper is sown, it must be sterilized on the outside, otherwise it would cause mould conditions in the flask, preventing germination.

The most important factor when sowing orchid seed is that of sterility; the next, which is also part of keeping sterile conditions, is that there should be no draughts in the sowing chamber. Commercial firms have laboratories made for the particular purpose of seed sowing, and these two essential factors are incorporated in the design, but a good many amateurs (and professionals) have succeeded

Table 2.1 Items essential for sowing orchid seed

- I Bunsen burner
- I Electric heater
- I Platinum loop (a loop set into a glass rod)
- I Test-tube about 15 cm (6 in) × 2 cm ($\frac{3}{4}$ in) standing in a heavier jar for stability and to keep it upright. (To hold the platform loop in surgical spirit)
- I Vial 8 cm (3 in) × 1.5 cm ($\frac{1}{2}$ in) for the sterilizing solution
- I Large pan with heating for water vapour
- I Table or bench for above
- I Autoclave or pressure cooker
- I Enamelled or stainless steel saucepan 20 cm (8 in) wide for boiling up and dissolving nutrients in flasks.
- 6 Flasks
- I Table or bench to hold flasks
- I Low-powered microscope
- I Box tissues

by adapting a kitchen or other living room.

First, the seed must be sterilized in such a manner that the seed case is free of contamination but the embryo is unharmed. To do this, the first step is to place a quantity of the seed, which has been kept in the paper, in the vial to not more than a quarter full. Then a sterilizing solution consisting of a suitable disinfectant is poured in and the vial shaken thoroughly to wet the outside of the dry seed. A wetting agent is helpful. After the seed has been thoroughly shaken, about ten minutes, the vial is left for a further five minutes. The solution is 10 g ($\frac{1}{3}$ oz) of calcium hypochlorite in 140 ml (5 fl. oz) of water. There are many others including sodium hypochlorite.

The nutrient solution, of which there is a big variety of formulae, is dissolved in water by boiling in the enamelled pan, and then poured into flasks of which by far the best is the Erlenmeyer, which has a wide base and is therefore stable, being shaped like a ship's decanter. The flasks are then put in the autoclave or pressure cooker, sterilized for fifteen or twenty minutes at a pressure of about I atm (15 lb/in²) and then cooled.

The platinum loop, which actually does the sowing, is placed in the test-tube filled with surgical spirit, the large pan is put over the heat,

just under simmering point, from the electric heater. The seed is left in its vial for fifteen minutes when it is time to innoculate the flasks.

From the bench where the sterilized and cooled flasks are standing, one is taken with the left hand and the vial in the same hand. The platinum loop is removed from the test-tube and, with the first and second fingers of the right hand, passed through the flame of the Bunsen burner; and the bung is removed from the flask with the fourth and fifth fingers of the right hand. The seed rises to the top of the fluid in the vial and forms a meniscus; the platinum loop scoops up seed and places it inside

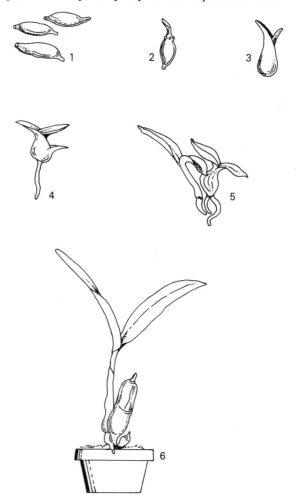

Germination of an orchid seed. I: seeds; 2: seedling, 4 months (I and 2 both greatly enlarged); 3: seedling, 7 months; 4: seedling, 12 months; 5: seedling, 18 months; 6: seedling, 2 years.

the flask on the surface of the nutrient solution which has cooled into a firm jelly. The loop is then passed again through the flame and back into its test-tube; the bung is replaced in the flask and the flask is then passed through the flame and the first flask is completed. The whole operation is performed over the pan of simmering water, and when the required number of flasks has been innoculated, aluminium foil is placed over each and secured with a rubber band. The flasks are then placed in subdued light for a period of weeks, paphiopedilum especially requiring longer than most, at least a month. The temperature at which the flasks are kept is $26.7°C$ ($80°F$) during the day to $21°C$ ($70°F$) at night. Gradually the light is increased but the tiny seedlings are very vulnerable, and should not be exposed to full light until they are transplanted, and even then should be given a further period of controlled light.

As soon as the seed have germinated (three to five weeks) they are then transplanted into fresh flasks by more or less the same procedure, except that the nutrient solution is stronger. This is termed 're-plating'. They then grow until they are sufficiently strong, with two or three leaves and tiny roots, to be put into pots or flats and kept in a warm part of the greenhouse. From there they graduate, first from a community pot or flat into a larger pot, sometime three to a pot, until they eventually finish up well on the way to maturity, with a large pot to themselves. Seedlings should always be kept on the move by being transplanted, otherwise they are apt to suffer a check to their growth.

Apical meristem method of propagation

The apical method of propagation was originally discovered through the efforts of scientists to discover a virus-free strain in plants other than orchids. It is applied to orchids as a means of obtaining a great number of plants, each individual being identical with the others particularly in colour, size, and shape of flower and in flowering season. It is a side-effect in orchids that plants produced by the meristem method are, at first, virus-free.

The method involves the same meticulous degree of sterility as that found in the successful innoculation of flasks, but cannot at present be used except where a genus includes plants having pseudobulbs—such as cattleyas, cymbidiums, odontoglossums, etc. The immature bud, or growth, at the base of the pseudobulb, should be about 2.5 cm (1 in) long and vigorous when it is cut off. It is placed under a, preferably, binocular microscope and stripped of its outermost leaves. It is sterilized for ten minutes in a 2% solution of calcium hypochlorite and then returned to the microscope where the rest of the leaves are removed to reveal the primordia, or the apical meristem, the first pair of leaves. This pair of leaves is then cut into several pieces and placed in Erlenmeyer flasks or test-tubes containing a liquid nutrient solution (i.e. without agar). The flask is sealed with a bung similar to that used when innoculating seed, and placed in a rotary shaker. This should be in a constant light of 100 foot candles and a constant temperature of $22°C$ ($72°F$). After two months the pieces of tissue, which have grown and are covered with what appear to be little protocorms, are removed, divided into about twenty pieces each, and replaced in fresh liquid nutrient solution. The process is repeated after a further two months and eventually the protocorms, by now numerous enough, are divided once more and placed on a nutrient solution containing agar (which becomes a firm jelly when cooled) and treated exactly as seedlings.

Other methods

The two laboratory methods of sowing orchid seed, the first of which has been in use for over fifty years, are not the simplest; the way orchid seed was sown before flasks and test-tubes were used, *was* simple. This was to take a plant growing vigorously and sow the seed on the surface of the compost. This was prepared to some extent by clipping the live sphagnum moss with sharp scissors so that its surface was smooth. The compost was moistened slightly first, if necessary, and the seed was tapped over it. It was then placed in a temperature of $21°C$ ($70°F$) during the day to $18.3°C$ ($65°F$) at night, and tended by usually one person, who watered it with extreme care with a fine watering can rose. When watering, the grower would cant the pot on its side. This was to prevent the seed from being washed into the compost and buried. A great deal of success attended these efforts because only the strongest seed germinated, and with regard to the number of potential seedlings in one orchid pod this was enough.

Another method of germinating orchid seed was to prepare a 13 cm (5 in) pot as follows. The pot would be boiled in water and then filled to 1.5 cm ($\frac{1}{2}$ in) below the rim with chopped live sphagnum moss, the surface of which was then clipped to make a smooth area. The material used for roller blinds was called, incorrectly, tiffany, but it was a coarsely woven soft type of hessian. A piece of this was boiled and when nearly dry was pushed over the moss tightly in a pot, and down the perimeter. The seed was sown on this surface in a glass case in a greenhouse kept at a day temperature of 26.6°C (80°F). A surprising number of seedlings were grown by this method, but again, it was the survival of the fittest, and the germination was nothing compared with that in a flask with the correct nutrient solution.

Composts
A brief review of the history of orchid composts

It may be interesting to review briefly the development of composts for orchids. Up to about 1890 the classic orchid compost was fibrous loam, fibrous peat, live sphagnum moss and charcoal. Although then, as now, orchid composts must be well drained, this must have been difficult to achieve with the materials available. A large plant would have had a smaller inverted pot placed in the base of its pot before potting in order to acquire better drainage, but the attempt to provide better drainage was evidenced by the typical orchid pot of clay being made with several holes at the sides and the bottom. This also allowed more freedom to the roots.

It was not, however, until polypodium fibre was introduced that a well drained compost became easier to mix. This is the root of *Polypodium vulgare*, derived from the Greek and meaning 'many little feet' from the appearance of the rhizome, its branches and roots. This required much labour to prepare, the rhizomes needing to be removed leaving only the roots, a tedious and indeed painful job, for the rhizome was like wire.

Polypodium was popular until about 1912 when osmunda fibre was discovered to be an excellent orchid compost. This is the root of *Osmunda regalis*, the royal fern, and it revolutionized the growing of orchids. It is obtainable from Maine, Florida, Canada, Japan and Europe and is expensive due to the labour involved in removing it from its habitat, usually dense bush. However, within the last years various barks have been discovered to be excellent substitutes for osmunda fibre. First to be used was redwood bark, from the *Sequoia*, which is relatively soft bark; then came various types of fir bark which were harder.

Most barks are by-products of the forestry industry which supplies pit-props for mines, timber for building and construction, boat building, etc.

The hardest bark of all is probably Corsican pine, which has the advantage of not breaking down quickly; indeed it can be used several times.

Whatever the ingredients of an orchid compost and wherever in the world the orchids are grown, the first essential is that the compost must be efficient for drainage. It cannot be too well drained, especially for epiphytes, but even the terrestrial genera are better grown in a compost which contains an ingredient to hold moisture temporarily but which releases it fairly quickly. Such additions to the mixture are bark of different kinds such as fir, redwood and tree-fern, osmunda fibre, charcoal and peat. Live sphagnum moss and various kinds of porous plastic hold moisture a little more than the barks etc., and the proportion may be increased when potting terrestrial orchids. Live sphagnum moss is not obtainable in all parts of the world where orchids are cultivated, more is the pity, but those orchid growers who do have access to it must count themselves very lucky; the others must put up with sphagnum moss peat which is a splendid substitute, but substitute it is.

Live sphagnum moss has a number of qualities, the most endearing of which is that it turns green when wet and white when dry, and is thus a perfect indicator for watering. It is mould-resistant, indeed it was used to dress wounds in the first world war in place of lint, which was scarce. When chopped (with the back of a saw) and put into a compost it still grows at the surface if regularly watered. If hard water is used regularly it does not grow and eventually dies, but if rain water or naturally lime-free water is employed at all times it thrives. It is useful for cattleyas and cymbidiums with osmunda fibre, but it is particularly useful for paphiopedilums. About the only pests which it attracts are springtails, *Collembola orchesella*, which are easy to get rid of by watering the plants with suitable insecticide when the compost is warm.

Bracken is a very useful material provided it is properly harvested, i.e. cut while still green and growing, and dried, just like the harvesting of hay.

Although orchids grown in different localities need different treatment, and it is necessary to be adaptable, a little experimentation quickly finds the right solution as regards the proportion of each ingredient in the composts but the proportions shown in Table 2.2 are recommended as a general guide.

Table 2.2 Orchid composts

Cattleya	*By volume*
Medium bark or chopped osmunda fibre	One half
Sphagnum moss (live)	One quarter
Charcoal and perlite or perlag ($\frac{1}{8}$ each)	One quarter
Cymbidium	
Harvested bracken chopped coarsely or medium bark or chopped osmunda fibre	One half
Sphagnum moss (live)	One quarter
Charcoal and perlite or perlag	One quarter
Miltonia, Odontoglossum, intergenerics	
Fine bark or finely chopped osmunda fibre	One half
Sphagnum moss (live)	One quarter
Fine charcoal and perlite or perlag	One quarter
Paphiopedilum and other terrestrials	
Medium bark or chopped osmunda fibre	One quarter
Sphagnum moss (fine) or moss peat	Three-quarters
Sprinkling of charcoal and perlite or perlag (a cupful per 4.55 l (1 gal))	
Phalaenopsis	
Chopped live sphagnum moss	Three-quarters
Perlite or perlag and charcoal	One quarter
Vanda	
Chopped live sphagnum moss	Three-quarters
Charcoal and perlite or perlag	One quarter

All the above orchids require a little coarse bone meal (*not* the powdered bone meal) and crocks or polystyrene at the bottom of the pot, up to about 5 cm (2 in), depending on the size of pot.

Containers and methods of utilizing them

For the potting of epiphytes, clay and plastic pots are in everyday use, but orchids, especially epiphytes, may with advantage be given their place of residence or habitat, in a variety of containers, including baskets of wickerwork; baskets made with teak or other wood, the bars of which are joined at the corners with copper wire. Even baskets made of clay; slabs of osmunda fibre, tree-fern fibre, or teak, apple or willow; or rafts of the same wood and of a size depending upon the shape and size of the plant to be housed, can be used. All epiphytes enjoy the freedom conferred by being suspended in a basket or on a slab; they are closer to the light and their roots are free to roam, absorbing moisture, and with it nutrients, from the air. In other words, they are as near to natural conditions as it is possible to be in the artificial confines of a greenhouse. It is mere convenience that they must, perforce, be grown on a bench. Ease of management, greater accessibility especially during watering or withdrawing a plant for use elsewhere and inspection for pests or disease all demand that the plants must be sited on a bench, but nevertheless the few which are chosen to be true 'air plants' are the lucky ones.

There are two kinds of clay pots, the hand-made, which are expensive, scarcer and far better than the others, the mass-produced nursery kind. The clay pot of the hand-made variety is porous and 'breathes' and consequently is more likely to give a congenial home to an orchid. The mass-produced type, being machine-made, requires a certain amount of oil in the clay to make the mixture cohere before it is cast and baked, and it thus becomes nearly as impervious as a tea-cup. It is also a poor design for orchids, being far too narrow at the base, especially for cattleyas and allied genera which are liable to be top-heavy when fully grown and in flower.

The plastic pot is greatly in demand and has

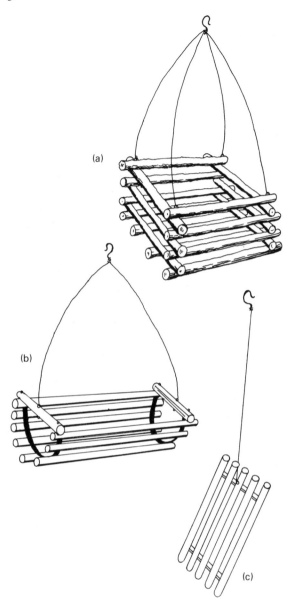

(a)

(b)

(c)

Different types of orchid containers. (a) Basket; (b) Boat; (c) Raft. The structures are made of wood—teak, apple or willow are all suitable—and are suspended by copper wire. For methods of construction see p. 34. In (c) the orchid is fastened to the raft by means of copper wire or nylon string.

been for several years, but again it is not designed for orchids and the narrowness at the base together with the lightness of present-day composts makes it unstable and likely to topple over when being

subjected to even a slight pressure from a hose when being watered. However, plastic pots are relatively cheap and, in spite of not being porous, are 'warmer' in cold conditions, and hold moisture more than the porous clay pot and are therefore better employed when dealing with terrestrial orchids. Adult paphiopedilums, however, can become top heavy but this is mitigated in their case by their being gregariously arranged on the bench—close to each other or 'pot thick'.

The ideal shape for an orchid pot, whether of clay or plastic, is shallower than the ordinary nursery pot, but a certain amount of effort in the way of detective work is usually necessary to track them down. The square plastic pot, is perhaps the best for seedlings in the small sizes and for paphiopedilums of all sizes for it is possible to arrange it on the staging closely. This makes for stability, but in any case the squareness renders it difficult to knock over.

The potting bench

As no soil is used today in orchid compost, bark being the modern compost, it might be thought unnecessary for the potting table or bench to be of especially heavy construction, because it is practically impossible to ram bark and charcoal into such a tight mass as it is with osmunda fibre when potting cattleyas and cymbidiums. The potting bench, however, should be solid and firm, the legs being of 10 × 10 cm (4 × 4 in) wood and the frame they support 8 × 2.5 cm (3 × 1 in). The table itself, which provides the platform for the work should be 2.5 × 10 cm (1 × 4 in) tongued and grooved (or similar solid wood), with a board of 5-ply or 6-ply, 13 or 15 cm (5 or 6 in) high on three sides so as to retain the compost. This table should be of the right height to work at comfortably while seated, say about 75 cm ((2½ ft) and about 90 or 120 cm (3 or 4 ft) wide, which is wide enough to take a supply of pots and the plants, or some of them, to be potted. If osmunda fibre is used a potting stick is necessary to tighten the compost while the plant is being repotted.

Potting, attaching to rafts, filling baskets

When potting epiphytes in either round or square

clay or plastic pots with one of the bark mixtures, a potting stick is not essential but it is useful. Previously the compost has been thoroughly mixed and dampened with rain water. This is very necessary because if the roots of a plant are potted in dry compost they will not immediately settle down, and furthermore, as newly potted plants are not watered for a week or two but given a daily freshening to the leaves with a spoon rose, this witholding of watering would be too much after potting with dry compost. Furthermore a really dry compost is difficult to moisten thoroughly, the water tending to run straight through the compost. A pot of the right size is selected, which means, in the case of a cattleya, one which will allow the plant to make another two growths. The plant normally makes one growth a year, starting in the spring and maturing by the autumn, and so the plant will not require to be repotted for a further two years. A cymbidium plant requires room for two growths too, but it is a little deceptive because the growths, developing into pseudobulbs, tend to become larger with each successive bulb and it may be found that the second pseudobulb does not have enough room. However, it is better to err on the conservative side because it only means potting at the end of a year instead of two, which is no hardship to a well grown plant. On this subject one of the crimes in orchid growing is to use too large a pot at repotting time, for the plant seems to become discouraged at the large space between its roots and the side of the pot, and does not produce its new roots so freely. This is true of all orchid plants, whether of the epiphytic or the terrestrial section.

Having selected the pot, a piece or two of polystyrene is placed in the bottom, and if available, some sphagnum moss across it. This combination of two materials makes for good drainage and at the same time limits the smaller particles of compost being washed through. The plant is then taken in the left hand (if right-handed) and held over the pot with the growths or pseudobulbs (or the rhizome) about level with the rim of the pot. The older pseudobulbs are then placed against the pot wall in such a manner that the youngest growth or pseudobulb is facing the centre. It will now be seen how the room for the two future growths is assessed. The plant is gently

handled until the potting is over; in particular the root system must be carefully treated. With the right hand, a quantity of compost is poured round the roots and on top of the sphagnum and polystyrene, ensuring that it is as evenly distributed as possible and that no gaps are left, then another handful is poured in and the pot gently tapped on the bench to allow the compost so far used, to settle down round the roots. After sufficient material has been used to fill the pot, a further gentle tapping on the bench will finish the operation. A label is inserted between the pot and the compost with details of the plant such as stud-book number or name, or if appropriate, the parents (in the case of a hybrid), date potted etc., and any other details required by the individual grower. If live sphagnum moss is available, a top dressing of this will prevent the light compost from floating over the side of the pot when watering and will act as a splendid watering guide (from its habit of turning white when dry, green when wet). The potted plant is then placed in a convenient receptacle, such as a tray or a sieve, before being put with the others on the staging in the orchid house.

Potting with osmunda fibre The preparations for using osmunda fibre are a little different. First it must be cleaned of all weeds, which do tend to grow quicker than the orchid and have an even quicker developing root system which will rob the compost of much of its goodness. Then the osmunda is chopped to the required size. An old fashioned chaff-cutter is ideal as it is adjustable for the length of fibre to be cut.

A potting stick is essential when potting with osmunda fibre, as it helps to firm the compost for cattleyas, cymbidiums, etc. The compost is then dampened and sieved or screened to remove the dust which would otherwise clog the compost and impair the qualities of drainage. The process is then repeated much as when potting with bark. The plant is held in the same position as before and the polystyrene and the sphagnum are put into the pot first. A little osmunda is picked up with the right hand, which is, at the same time, holding the potting stick, and then pressed round the plant's roots by the potting stick. When sufficient compost is placed in the pot, the potting stick's final task is to be inserted between the compost and the wall of the pot, and down its side, and pressed towards the centre, the gap made being filled with more osmunda. This is repeated while rotating the pot until the compost is firm or tight enough.

For seedlings and small plants, the ingredients of the compost are the same, but are finer the smaller the plant. For instance, in potting, say, small cymbidiums just out of the flask, the compost consists of osmunda (if used) put through an 0.16 cm ($\frac{1}{8}$ in) sieve, live sphagnum moss rubbed through the same diameter sieve, fine charcoal and perlag of the finest grade. A little more sphagnum moss than is used in the potting of adult plants and a little less osmunda fibre is used in seedling composts of all kinds.

Potting Paphiopedilum and other terrestrial orchids Adult paphiopedilums and other terrestrial orchids require to be potted in a mixture which, although well drained, is still capable of retaining moisture, and this is effected by altering the proportion of the ingredients; rather less of the bark or osmunda fibre, and more of the live sphagnum moss, or sphagnum moss peat. The mixture is made and then dampened with rain water or other lime-free water. The polystyrene and live sphagnum moss are placed in the bottom of the pot which, for convenience, is a square plastic one, or of porous clay. A paphiopedilum does not have pseudobulbs, but the oldest growth is placed at the back of the pot (in potting cattleya and cymbidium the oldest pseudobulb is to the back) and the newest growth facing towards the centre. A little bark is placed over the polystyrene and the sphagnum and the roots carefully placed on them after having had a little compost gently inserted among them. The base of the plant should be level with the rim of the pot or just slightly below it. In the case of paphiopedilums and other terrestrial orchids a top dressing of live sphagnum moss is helpful for a number of reasons.

If osmunda is available it should be chopped a little smaller than when used for adult epiphytes and the potting should not be finished off by tightening so much. It should be firm but not compressed.

The top dressing recommended for terrestrial orchids is not out of place for any orchids, especially when potted in fine bark, because this has a tendency to float over the rim of the pot. A good layer of live sphagnum moss prevents this, helps maintain a little local humidity round the plant and improves the appearance.

Hanging containers When using a wicker basket for potting orchids to be suspended from the roof, copper wire or nylon string should be used, in the case of a square basket attached to each corner, and with a round one, three separate lengths attached at equal distances round the rim of the basket and both the square and the round baskets having a hook or ring at the apex of the wire to suspend the basket.

The roots of the plant to be put in the basket should be carefully cleaned of all old compost and a bed of sphagnum moss placed on the base of the inside of the basket. No drainage material is required as the wickerwork is sufficiently open to allow for thorough draining. The rest of the compost is then poured round the plants in the same manner as in the case of the other plants described. A square basket made of wood (teak is one of the best), consists of bars or rods of wood to make a basket of the required size, say 15 cm (6 in). The bars are about 2 cm ($\frac{3}{4}$ in) each side and 15 cm (6 in) long. A hole is drilled through each bar exactly 2.5 cm (1 in) from each end through which

Slatted basket with orchid showing how this type of container allows roots to develop freely and affords excellent drainage for the compost.

to thread the wire, and a 'stop' used for the bottom bar. First a small 'raft' is made with a 15-cm (6-in) bar at each end and five 15-cm (6-in) bars nailed to them on top by copper nails. The copper wire is then threaded through the corners of the raft, and bars placed on the top of the raft and threaded with the copper wire alternately with the previous bars until enough, say three or four, make a basket of sufficient depth for the purpose. It is as well not to make a raft too large, for reasons of space, and because a plant must not be potted in too large a pot.

Rafts A raft made of teak (the first stage of the basket), is a natural home for air plants, consisting as it does of five bars 15 cm (6 in) long nailed with copper wire to two cross bars 15 cm (6 in) long. Copper wire is fastened to one of the cross bars and attached to a nail, screw or hook in a glazing bar, purlin or other beam in the roof of the greenhouse. It will not be horizontal but will hang down almost vertically.

A basket which is efficient but which is not seen much unless specially made, and which used to be popular for suspending from the roof of a greenhouse, is one made of clay. This is shallow and is ideal for smaller epiphytes such as *Coelogyne cristata*. It is long-lasting and serves the same purpose as one made of wood.

When using a raft or log for housing epiphytes the plant is fastened to the raft, log or slab by means of copper wire or nylon string. A bed of live sphagnum moss is first placed on the raft etc., and the plant then placed on this, care being taken to avoid damaging the rhizome by tying too tightly. The raft, log or slab should be thoroughly moistened before the plant is attached to it. This is to encourage root action as soon as possible.

Watering requirements

Before discussing the watering of plants it would be as well to explain a pitfall which can cause a great amount of unnecessary work and make the watering of orchid plants more complex than it ought to be. This error is to arrange (or stage) plants having heterogeneous composts mixed together on the same bench. Plants potted in bark mixture should not be put with those in osmunda and sphagnum moss. To go further, plants which have been potted in clay pots should not be mixed together in a haphazard way with plants potted in plastic pots. To make orchid-growing life even easier, pots of roughly the same size should be staged together. The reason is plain to see after having fallen into the trap, for the plants potted in a bark mixture will dry out quicker than those in osmunda and those in clay much quicker than those in plastic. The rate of evaporation is so much faster in porous clay pots than in plastic ones that watering in spring and summer has to be more frequent. This is not at all injurious to the plants, but naturally causes more work. It goes without saying that epiphytes are better grown in separate houses from terrestrial orchids, if possible, from several points of view. To take a quick example, cattleya hybrids compared with paphiopedilum hybrids need more light, less water and humidity. Paphiopedilums are gregarious plants and enjoy being closely staged but cattleyas should be put further apart from each other on the bench or staging so that each plant is able to have as much light and air as possible.

One more important point to observe is that rainwater, or naturally soft water, both lime-free, are beneficial to orchids, but not water which has gone through a water-softener. This process changes the calcium in the water to sodium; sodium is even more deleterious to orchids than calcium.

Watering covers a multitude of different functions for which each should have an appropriate implement or attachment to an implement. The best and most efficient is the watering can with a long spout and a variety of roses to fix to the end. The roses are of different shapes, sizes and have different sized perforations. For watering small seedlings these perforations must be the finest and a useful gadget to use with this rose is a strainer or filter through which to pass the water in order to prevent particles of detritus from clogging the perforations. The old-fashioned metal watering-cans used with brass roses are probably the best, and are fitted with a filter inside the can at the base of the spout, but these filters are usually too coarse (because the can is used with many different roses) and allows bits of rubbish to pass through to end up by clogging a fine rose.

For everyday use, a round rose with coarse

perforations is useful, and to make it capable of directing a stream of water on to the surface of the compost of individual plants, the centre of the perforated plate can be gently pressed in, leaving it slightly concave. This has the effect of concentrating the water to where it is needed and of avoiding wetting adjacent plants if they are not due to be watered.

The spoon rose, a usually larger rose and oval in shape (like a spoon) has coarser perforations than the round one, and has quite a different function. It has a spreading pattern and covers a greater area and it is not used, consequently, for selective watering, but to dampen the foliage on those occasions when the inside temperature is too high, usually during the summer months. It is used, too, with a different action from the normal rose, and is flicked quickly over the plants, taking care that each has its quota of water. A reduction in the air temperature is the result, and, much more important, a lowering of the leaf temperature.

Other and quicker but not better ways of watering are the overhead irrigation systems and watering by the use of a hose attached to a tap, mostly used where there is soft mains water and consequently adequate water pressure. An overhead system consists of lines of metal or plastic piping running the length of the orchid house and with nozzles of varying coarseness at intervals. The system relies on an efficient water pressure and sufficient water (either mains water or rain, pond or river water, or water caught from the roof of the orchid house and directed by down-pipes into rainwater tanks in the greenhouse). This water is collected from each house and pumped up into a main overhead tank for distribution to the various houses, or a particular house, when necessary. This system may not be necessary when the mains water (or city water) is free of lime and other toxic elements, is plentiful and of sufficient pressure. If it is plentiful and lime free but not of sufficient pressure, the large overhead tank is necessary, and if high enough up will provide the pressure itself without the use of a pump. The system is useful where the nursery is large and the staff, as is sometimes the case, not big enough or is not skilled enough, but it has its disadvantages. It cannot be used for selective watering, i.e. watering those plants which need to be watered and leaving the others severely alone, which is the ideal way. 'It droppeth as the gentle rain from heaven upon the place beneath'—and this might not be the right place.

As well as the time of year for watering, copiously in summer, restrained in winter, the time of day is of equal if not more importance. This is because the plants give out water during the hours of darkness and take it up during the daytime, the process of transpiration. The plants also take up carbon dioxide during the hours of daylight and give out oxygen, reversing the process during the hours of darkness during which hours the plant makes its growth. The watering of the plants should therefore take place when they are receptive, i.e. in the hours of daylight, furthermore it should have most effect after the atmosphere has warmed up, particularly in the winter months. During the summer, when the sun rises early watering can also be executed earlier. This regime applies particularly to the temperate zones where orchids must be grown under glass. In the subtropics and in the tropics they can in most cases be grown on suitable sites outside, and the only protection needed is a shelter to prevent rain from damaging flowers.

Probably the second best method of watering orchids (the best being the watering can) and one which contains the best of both methods, is by a 1.5 cm ($\frac{1}{2}$-in) hose, attached at one end to a tap, provided the water is lime-free. At the other end is a watering lance, similar to the spout on the can, which is machined to take a brass rose and a device to regulate the flow of water from just a trickle for seedlings and small plants to a full flow for large adult plants. The type of compost has a bearing on the force of water which is feasible as fine bark and polyurethane are inclined to float off over the rim of the pot, to be washed away, if the force is too great.

If the city water is not lime-free, the rain water in the tank must be relied on and an electric centrifugal pump with a suction hose in the water and a delivery hose leading to the watering lance is essential. This obviates the tedious task of making frequent trips to the tank to refill the can, and the regulating device enables the operator to give just the right flow of water to suit the plants he is watering.

When to water

There is no hard and fast rule for when to water. The answer is to water when the plant needs it, and this is difficult to determine. If live sphagnum moss is part of the compost it is much easier, for the live moss growing on the top will turn white when the compost is dry, but the bark mixtures are inclined to dry out quickly on the surface while the rest of the compost is moist. This is why the previous remarks on staging the plants are important, for if the plants dry out at roughly the same rate, a moisture indicator may be inserted into the compost of sample plants, taken at random, to determine the average needs of the plants in that house. A good rule is, when in doubt leave for a day. One of the reasons for not using hard water is that it kills the moss.

The use of the hose with the watering lance method is more flexible than the overhead irrigation because the watering lance is adaptable to take various nozzles such as a mister, or a fogger or a coarser mister for foliar feeding. When using a mister on the lance, with a solution of one of the formulae for foliar feeding, the suction hose must be withdrawn from the rainwater tank and placed in a large, portable container holding the fertilizer. The misting nozzle uses but a fraction of the volume of water that a rose on the end of the watering arm does. In addition to feeding the plants the lance is very useful for various insecticides, with the appropriate nozzle, especially the fog nozzle. Some of the most effective insecticides, however, are dangerous if inhaled and a simple respirator should always be used.

Plants on rafts, slabs and in baskets can be mist-sprayed both with fertilizer and with insecticide, but when they are to be watered thoroughly they should be immersed in a bucket of water.

Fertilizer requirements

The modern bark composts, with polystyrene and charcoal among other ingredients, are almost completely sterile, and osmunda fibre is nearly so. They provide no nutrients for the plant and so these have to be provided by the grower. The spring and summer are the main months in which to feed, tapering off for the autumn and winter.

The use of fertilizers for orchids has become much less dangerous for, when osmunda fibre was the most popular ingredient in mixtures, the fertilizers used in those days caused a build-up of salts which were toxic after a time. The procedure was to water with fertilizer about twice a month and, in between the applications of fertilizer, the plants were watered with normal water, thus leaching the salts safely away.

The highly scientific modern fertilizers have been evolved over a period and are now quite safe, and, moreover are so carefully balanced that they supply an exact answer to any orchid plant's needs. In addition, the use of foliar feeding has become better known, and as the fertilizer does not enter the compost but is misted on to the leaves, there is no danger of toxic salts building up at the base of the compost.

There are foliar fertilizers to suit every need, from the 30.10.10 for small plants and seedlings to the 18.18.18 for adult plants. For feeding a plant in the bud stage there is even one, 10.30.20, to induce better flowering. It is still better to give a very dilute solution of foliar feed every day in the spring and summer than to give a strong (normal) dose of ordinary fertilizer once a month, between ordinary waterings. Even paphiopedilums appreciate a foliar feed.

A typical example of a foliar fertilizer for general use is:

Nitrogen (N)	22%
Phosphoric acid	(P_2O_5) 21%
Potash (K_2O)	17%

together with the essential trace elements, iron, magnesium, manganese, copper, cobalt, boron, zinc and molybdenum. Therefore the first example given above is nitrogen 30%, phosphorous 10% and potash 10%.

Lighting requirements

Of three factors necessary for good orchid growing, light, heat and humidity, each of which is equally important, the primus inter pares is light. Each factor has to be carefully balanced with the others and alteration in any one of them throws the others out of kilter. Having regard to the divergent habitats of the various genera and species of orchids, some of which are found growing at sea level in the full blaze of the tropical sun and others being content in the shade of trees or rocks at 3000–4500 m (10–15000 ft) elevation, it is important to realise that orchids, even species within the same genus, require different growing conditions. In the artificial confines of a greenhouse the aim must be to attain conditions which are approximate to their natural growing conditions.

The problems concerning light and heat are not so pressing near the sub-tropics—the nearer to the equator the more the problems change to those of shading and cooling. For instance, regions like the west coast of California and the Sydney district of New South Wales are able to grow cymbidiums in the open air with but a covering of saran cloth overhead to help keep the flowers from being spoilt by the rain, but cattleyas can be grown in Florida, Durban and Queensland by the same method whereas cymbidiums and odontoglossums prove difficult. The further north in the northern hemisphere and naturally the colder the winters the less natural light is available and the more artificial heat is required.

Iceland at 70° north must be the most favoured orchid growing country, albeit in artificial conditions, because the greenhouse (and the dwelling houses too) are heated by hot water from the geysers and the electricity is provided by hydro-electric installations and is relatively inexpensive. There is also an abundance of water. The only fly in the ointment is the six hours of daylight during the six months of winter. The orchid growers there have to black out for twelve to fourteen hours in the summer and conversely give their plants ten to twelve hours light in the winter from the cheap electricity. A welcome side-effect is that the long, cold winter inhibits the proliferation of harmful insects, although clegs or horse-flies are a serious pest on the salmon rivers.

Light is measured in horticulture by foot-candles. It means that a candle placed a foot above an object gives an intensity on that object of one foot candle. On a dull winter's day in the temperate regions the light at noon in a greenhouse reaches an intensity of about four hundred foot candles. A healthy cymbidium plant requires around three thousand foot candles during the summer, but it receives much more in the Mediterranean types of climate as in southern California or New South

Wales, and a much higher average than four hundred all during the year.

To measure the foot candles, a light meter is required, and these are expensive, but an ordinary photographic meter is sufficient. Proceed as follows. Place a clean piece of writing paper, or several sheets of white typing paper, on the surface to be measured. If typing paper is to be used it should be at least four sheets in thickness.

Set the film speed at an ASA rating of 10. Hold the meter pointed at the centre of the white surface at least as close as the smaller dimension of this surface. If the white paper is 30 × 35 cm (12 × 14 in) the meter should be at least 30 cm (12 in) from the surface. Do not cast a shadow on any part of the white surface, as this will give incorrect results. Table 2.3 will convert the meter reading from f/stops a 100th and 1/60th second directly in footcandles.

Table 2.3. Lighting requirements

1/100 sec	1/60th sec	Footcandles
f/3.5	f/4.5	400
f/4	f/5	500
f/4.5	f/5.6	650
f/5	f/6.3	800
f/5.6	f/7	1000
f/7	f/9	1300
f/8	f/10	2000
f/9	f/11	2400
f/10	f/12.7	3200
f/11	f/14	4000
f/12.7	f/16	5200
f/14	f/18	6400

(From Dr. Sidney A. Schwartz. Reprinted in *Orchid Review* from *Orchidata* (1961), **1** (5). September).
(*Editor's note.* For Grolux tubes multiply above result by 18 for correct footcandle reading).

There are three different rays from the sun: heat rays, light rays and actinic rays. These are different according to their wave length, but the most necessary ones for the life processes of plants are the light and the actinic rays. Radiant energy is reflected from solid surfaces and consequently loss is lessened by the reflection. This is one reason why the inside of a greenhouse should be painted white, or metallic paint such as aluminium should be used.

The greater the intensity of light in a greenhouse, the higher the humidity and heat must be to keep the three factors in balance, hence the necessity to arrange separate sections, or to have separate greenhouses for the requirements of different orchids. It will be found that often the plants which require high light intensity also require a higher heat, although this is not always so as there are many which need high light and intermediate to cool temperatures such as cymbidiums. It is also a significant factor that situations in the sub-tropics and tropics receive all the light that orchids demand, having from ten hours' light all through the year in the sub-tropics to twelve hours' light and twelve of darkness in the tropics.

The importance of shading

The light too, as well as being much longer in hours, is of a greater intensity, and the question of shading orchid houses is of major importance. Of course, the importance of this shading is not confined to the tropics and sub-tropics, for, in the summer even in temperate climates, it is very necessary to have appropriate shading for most, if not all, orchids, and especially for the terrestrial orchids such as paphiopedilum hybrids and species.

There are several different kinds of shading, the most simple but not the most efficient being liquid shading, applied at the beginning of the spring and removed in the autumn. Its great disadvantage is that on dull days it cannot be removed and replaced and on those days during the spring and autumn it cannot be rolled up like a blind to leave the glass clear. Although there are substances, in concentrated liquid or in water-soluble powder form, which are easily and quickly applied with a paint-sprayer, it is a different matter when the time comes in the autumn to remove them. The best of these horticultural shading materials are those which gradually deteriorate with the weather, and after a summer's rain and sun, are thinned, thus letting light through during the summer progressively, but even these involve cleaning the glass before the winter.

The roller-type blinds of wooden slats or of cloth are mounted on rails which run horizontally along the house. The rails are 15 cm (6 in) from the glass and if slats are used these should be about 2.5 cm (1 in) apart. These horizontal blinds are easier to instal than those running from the ridge to the gutters as they do not require ropes and pulleys.

The shading in the cymbidium regions of Southern California are of saran cloth and keep the mid-day sun from striking directly down on to the plants. It is a simple arrangement something like a fruit cage consisting of uprights supporting horizontal laths on which the cloth is fastened. The sides are usually open. This arrangement is, of course, not suitable for those regions which have a cold winter.

Heating requirements: cool, intermediate and warm greenhouses

The orientation of an orchid house is thought to be best if it is north by south, but this depends on the particular location and latitude. With high ground or forest to the east or west to obscure the rising and setting sun, the orchid house would possibly be better sited with the length facing the south to take advantage of as much light during the day as possible, with of course, adequate shading, to shield the plants from the sun at noon.

A span house running from north to south is the best because the sun will give all the plants an equal amount of hours of light. In early morning in summer, and until about noon it will warm the plants on the east side and the plants on the west in the afternoon, and for about four hours covering mid-day it will irradiate the whole length of the house equally, the ridge and the glazing bars providing some extra shade. A house running east to west would not allow each side to receive an equal amount of light and warmth particularly if it is wide enough for a central bench with tiering to be installed. The north side of this house would not receive so much light as the south.

Orchid houses are variable in size and proportion, but the most efficient have proved to be relatively narrow, and, because of the cost of heating, relatively low, not much more than 3.3 m (11 ft) high.

However, many orchid establishments, mostly in eastern USA have been growing orchids, particularly cattleyas, in houses up to the dimensions of 75 × 13.5 × 9 m (250 × 50 × 30 ft), but most of these houses were built when energy was not so expensive. For seedling houses and for terrestrial orchids, a low roof allowing a high natural humidity is essential.

The heating of commercial houses is by means of hot water pipes from a boiler, the pipes being under the staging on each side. The boiler burns solid fuel, oil or gas or is electrically heated. Each of these has advantages over the others and the choice depends on availability and cost. The pipes, too, vary from 10 cm (4 in) cast iron or cast steel, to 4 cm ($1\frac{1}{2}$ in) steel pipes. A comparison of these pipes is shown in Table 2.4.

Table 2.4 Comparison of capacities and heating surfaces between six pipes of 4 cm ($1\frac{1}{2}$ in) diameter and two pipes of 10 cm (4 in) diameter

No of pipes and diameter	Per 18 m (60 ft) run of 4 cm ($1\frac{1}{2}$ in) and 10 cm (4 in) diameter pipes		
	Absolute volume	Volume of water	Heating surface area
6 pipes of: 4 cm ($1\frac{1}{2}$ in) diam.	125 121 cm³ (7634 in³)	125 litres (27.5 gal)	13.13 m² (20 358 in²)
2 pipes of: 10 cm (4 in) diam.	296 577 cm³ (18 095 in³)	298 litres (65.5 gal)	11.67 m² (18.095 in²)

From above it will be seen that by using 6 pipes of 4 cm ($1\frac{1}{2}$ in) instead of 2 pipes of 10 cm (4 in) there is a $12\frac{1}{2}\%$ increase in the heating surface using 42% of the water in the 10 cm (4 in) pipes, and 4.55 l (1 gal) of water in the 4 cm ($1\frac{1}{2}$ in) pipes heats 740 in² of heating surface, but that in the 10 cm (4 in) pipes it heats only 277 in².

The only advantage of 10 cm (4 in) pipes apparently is that they retain heat a little longer if the boiler ceases to function. In all other respects the 4 cm ($1\frac{1}{2}$ in) pipes win. The pipes themselves are cheaper and all the accompaniments and fittings such as screw-down, check or motorized valves, brackets etc., are very much less expensive. The water, being of less volume is circulated more

rapidly by the pump on the boiler, thus being more responsive to thermostatic control, and of course, for the same reason uses less fuel. The heating surface which is what matters most, is heated more rapidly and the water temperature in the flow pipes is equivalent to that in the return.

When installing a boiler and pipes, it is wise to have a boiler bigger than is thought necessary and, if anything, too many pipes rather than just sufficient, for these reasons. Firstly it is mechanically erroneous to 'drive' a boiler and if the boiler is only just big enough, or a little under capacity, it will need to be 'driven' on occasions. Secondly, a large number of pipes means a low water temperature needed in the pipes to maintan a required air temperature with consequently a better atmosphere for the plants. The worst crime in heating an orchid house is to overheat the pipes in order to acquire an air temperature two or three degrees higher and succeeding only by reducing the humidity so much that a dry 'feel' is in the air.

The benches or staging on which the plants are to be placed should be about 83 cm ($2\frac{3}{4}$ ft) high and about 1.05 m ($3\frac{1}{2}$ ft) or 1.13 m ($3\frac{3}{4}$ ft) wide. It is false economy to have the staging greatly wider than this because it makes the plants in the back two rows difficult to see for watering and to retrieve when needed. The staging is made of wood slats, cedar being the best wood from its longlasting qualities, but heavy gauge galvanized mesh-metal lasts longer. However, it is a less natural material than wood, and is colder.

There is a sub-stage underneath the plant stage, designed to hold some moisture holding material such as coke or breeze, shingle, leytag (expanded clay) etc. This is to provide humidity and should be kept constantly wet, otherwise the heat from the pipes would dry out the base of the pots and cause damage. However, one of the reasons for having plentiful piping, either 10 cm (4 in) or 4 cm ($1\frac{1}{2}$ in), is that the water temperature, as explained before, does not need to be so high as when just an adequate amount of piping is installed. For instance, if there is only sufficient piping to keep a temperature 18.3°C (65°F) during the day, with a water heat of, say 49°C (120°F), by having more piping the lower water temperature will keep this air temperature even and so the sub-staging will not be necessary, indeed it will itself absorb some of the heat which should be used to heat the atmosphere.

There have been occasions when the hot water pipes have been suspended over the benches, and this has been successful, but is not recommended, for, apart from the hot air rising to where it is not wanted, at the apex of the roof, the pipes themselves (they were 10 cm (4 in)) obscure essential light, especially during the dull days of winter.

Cool orchid houses

The orchids from the High Andes, the Cordilleras and the Himalayas, together with mountains like the North Bornean Mount Kinabalu require commensurately cool conditions. The difference between a cool orchid house and a greenhouse used for other plants is mainly a matter of temperature, and temperature must accord with the requirements of the inmates. An ordinary greenhouse is used for plants to be set out in the garden in the spring and these plants are merely wintered in the greenhouse and do not make much growth while there, which is why the winter night temperature can go down to $1.7°C (35°F)$ without doing the plants any harm, with a day temperature of $7°C (45°F)$ or less. A cool orchid house, on the other hand, being the home of tropical plants, albeit from the cool places of the tropics, needs minimum night temperatures of around $4.5°C (40°F)$ for a couple of months in deepest winter, rising gradually to $14°C (57°F)$ in the three summer months. The day temperatures are the higher forties up to $10°C (50°F)$ in the winter to $18°C (64°F)$ in the summer. It is easier to maintain the minimum temperatures in the winter by pipe heat than to keep the summer temperatures down to $18°C (64°F)$. There should always be a difference of $3°–8°C (5°–15°F)$ between the day and the night temperatures.

The day-time summer temperatures are kept down as much as possible by means of the ventilators in the roof, by shading and by the use of electric fans. Evaporative cooling is useful for all three types of orchid growing: cool, intermediate and warm. Electric extractor fans are set into the wall at intervals of about 9 m (30 ft), and set into the wall on the opposite side are apertures of about 90 cm (3 ft) in diameter. These apertures are covered with straw, or thick cloth and this is constantly wetted by a trickle of water from a tank, well or other supply activated by a pump with a delivery hose leading to the apertures. The extractor fans draw the air in from the wet material covering the apertures across the house and the temperature is lowered by $5°–8°C (10°–15°F)$. The surplus water, after wetting the straw, is returned to the tank or well by a hose set into a container beneath the aperture. This system enables cooler growing species and hybrids to be grown in a district which otherwise would be too warm for them. The costly systems of air conditioning have been very successful in the cultivation of orchids by amateurs but they are not really for the commercial grower.

A further method of regulating the humidity and temperature is that of underbench irrigation, and this consists of lines of tubing with nozzles every $0.9–1.2$ m (3–4 ft). The misting nozzles are more easily cleaned than those overhead, which, although frequently used with misting nozzles, are more practical when fitted with coarser ones the effect of which is roughly equivalent to watering with a spoon rose. The primary purpose of the coarser nozzles is to moisten the leaves of the plants and thus to reduce the leaf temperature.

This system is wasteful of water as the spray is indiscriminate and reaches every place within its orbit: the plants, the paths and the benches, but this raises the humidity and lowers the temperature and is a blessing in disguise.

In recent years ventilators in the side wall of an orchid house have been unfashionable, especially in temperate to cold districts. The ventilation through the roof, sometimes by the assistance of fans, has always been the method by which stale or overheated air is allowed to escape, but the cool house is a little different from the others, and side ventilators in this house are usually found in most establishments. In the warmer regions, of course, side ventilation is a necessity.

In particular, the odontoglots require the buoyant atmosphere supplied by side and top ventilators, together with more shading and humidity.

The cool house is the home for many orchids of divergent need. The Colombian miltonias and odontoglossums, some of the paphiopedilum species such as *P. venustum, P. insigne* and *P. villosum; Coelogyne crisata, Oncidium forbesii, O.*

ornithorhynchum, Pleione lagenaria and many more may be grown in the cool house. Some may need more light than others, and some may require a shady spot on the staging. The epiphytes needing more light should be hung near the glass.

Intermediate orchid houses

Probably more orchids are grown in the intermediate house than in any other, because orchids generally are adaptable plants and are able to survive under conditions that are by no means optimum. Furthermore, young plants, which are called by orchid growers *unflowered seedlings*, although some are adult plants which have not yet flowered, need a little more heat than when they become adults and consequently the cool-growing orchids, when young, can be housed in the intermediate house; indeed they can even do better there. The heating requirements generally in the intermediate house are just that little higher. The converse, however, is not so true, and plants requiring an intermediate regime would not be so likely to thrive in cool conditions, especially during the winter.

The winter night temperatures are $10°C$ ($50°F$) to $11°C$ ($52°F$) during the three months or so of cold weather to $13°C$ ($55°F$) during the day, and in the summer months the temperatures are night $16°C$ ($61°F$) and day $22°C$ ($72°F$). These are not average temperatures or maximum or minimum but guide lines. On a hot summer's day, for instance, with the temperature outside at $32°C$ ($90°F$) in the shade, even with roller blinds, ventilators open and fans going continually (unless of the evaporative cooling variety) the temperature will still climb to $26.6°C$ ($80°F$) to $29°C$ ($85°F$), in the intermediate house. Above this the danger mark is reached, for leaf temperature will become too high and yellowing of the foliage follows. To prevent this is simple, and a hose with a spoon rose attached to it and quickly flicked over the leaves will soon cool them and, in addition, lower the air temperature. An overhead sprinkler system as described previously is of great use during the summer if only to keep the temperature down.

All greenhouses have a warmer end, although this is less so when an efficient circulating pump is installed for this evens up the water temperature; plants which need a little extra heat should be staged here, the warmer end.

A whole wide world of orchids is suitable for the intermediate house: cattleyas, which require as much light without making the leaves warm; cymbidiums, which need light too and as much as cattleyas, but require a little more watering and should be placed at the cooler end of the house; paphiopedilum species (most of them) and hybrids (all of them), the species *P. parishii*, *P. philippinense* and *P. spiceranum* being illustrated elsewhere in this book; most oncidiums, dendrobiums and some vandas; all these and many more are at home in the intermediate house.

Warm orchid houses

Formerly called the East India house, or stove house the warm house lives up to its name. Winter temperatures are even more critical in the warm house than in either of the others. During this period night temperatures, with the correct humidity, must be kept to a minimum of $14°C$ ($57°F$) for three or four months and the day temperatures $16°C$ ($61°F$) to $18°C$ ($64°F$). These may not seem too dramatic during a hot summer but it involves burning much midnight oil to keep them up to these figures on a freezing winter night. This fact is the reason for the warm house orchids not being grown in temperate climates so much as the other orchids available. Only those growers living in climates in or near to the sub-tropics can hope to have success with these plants with a carefree attitude and no heating worries. The problems in those regions are not those of heating, as remarked on elsewhere, but of keeping the temperatures down to reasonable levels. There is also a much greater hazard in insects proliferating, consequently, from familiarity, these growers are experts in pestology.

There is an enticing variety of species and, nowadays, hybrids suitable for the warm house. *Phalaenopsis* and the vandaceous species and hybrids, bred for the most part in the Far East but also in Hawaii, Florida and California are fit subjects for this house, together with some paphiopedilums such as *P. bellatulum*, *P. callosum*, *P. hirsutissimum*, *P. hookerae* and others, even some cymbidiums such as *C. finlaysonianum* and *C.*

madidum and its hybrid *C.* Francis Hunt and, from the old world, *Cattleya aclandiae, C. rex* and *Rhyncolaelia digbyana* and its variety *fimbripetala.*

The vandas may be suspended near the roof, as they require as much light as possible without burning the leaves, but, due to their natural habitats at high altitudes, *Vanda amesiana, V. coerulea* and *V. cristata* require cooler conditions and should be in the intermediate house.

A high temperature, high humidity and plenty of light should be the rule, therefore, with direct sunlight shaded from the phalaenopses and the paphiopedilums.

Air/relative humidity; need for air circulation

Even the terrestrial orchids require a constant change of air to enable them to complete their cycle of growth and for epiphytes it is, if possible, even more vital. The life of orchids, like that of all phanerogamous plants depends on the regular intake of carbon dioxide during the hours of daylight through the stomata on the underside of their leaves and, in the case of cattleyas, vandas, phalaenopses and many others through their aerial roots. This carbon dioxide, together with other plant nutrients present in the air, is rendered available to the plant when conditions such as relative humidity, temperature and of course, light are in balance. The plant in these conditions gives out oxygen. During the hours of darkness the process is reversed, the carbon having already changed into starch is turned into sugar which is used by the plant in the process of forming cells. It is, therefore, of the utmost importance for relative humidity and temperature to be balanced with light during the daylight hours. During the hours of darkness temperature and humidity are lowered, which is one of the reasons why orchid plants should not be watered nor should mist sprays be employed late in the afternoon.

If there is a danger of the temperature in the orchid house in question being accidentally lowered, either from mechanical failure or other causes, it is better to refrain from giving any water or irrigation during that day. In extremely cold weather dry plants will suffer less than if moist.

Air circulation is important, apart from cooling the leaves, for the reason that carbon dioxide is heavier than air and consequently a gentle circulation will distribute it to every part of the house, and especially to the leaves. This is, of course true of the heating as well, a system of 90 cm (3 ft) diameter fans set horizontally under the apex of the roof and rotating very slowly will push the warmer air downwards and a lower water temperature in the pipes will be required. It also, if the ventilators are opened, draws fresh air in during hot days and thus lowers the house temperature.

The evaporative cooling system described before, is perhaps the best of both worlds as it provides relative humidity together with a regulating of the temperature.

The maxim that orchids need fresh air but not draughts is one always to be born in mind.

Reproduction by division

The time to divide a mature plant is when new growth is just beginning, or a little before. Cattleyas, miltonias, cymbidiums, oncidiums, epidendrums and other orchids with clearly defined pseudobulbs are relatively simple to propagate by division.

To take the cattleya first, and a typical plant of, say, eight pseudobulbs, the oldest two being without leaves. The first four are selected for the main plant and the two remaining with leaves plus the two leafless ones, called the 'back piece', are severed by cutting between the two pieces or divisions, down through the rhizome. The important point to make is that it must be ensured that there is a 'live eye' at the base of the leading pseudobulb of the back division. This 'live eye' is a recessed bud low down at the base of the pseudobulb. There are two such buds on the *front* pseudobulb of a cattleya, one of which, usually, makes a break or growth, which eventually becomes a pseudobulb itself. Nature has ensured the continuance of the plant because, if the new young growth is broken off or damaged severely, the remaining one takes over and starts to grow. Frequently both buds start, in which case the plant is without a reserve bud, in the unlikely event of both growths being broken.

If the live eye on the leading pseudobulb of the back division is really live, all is well, but if it is

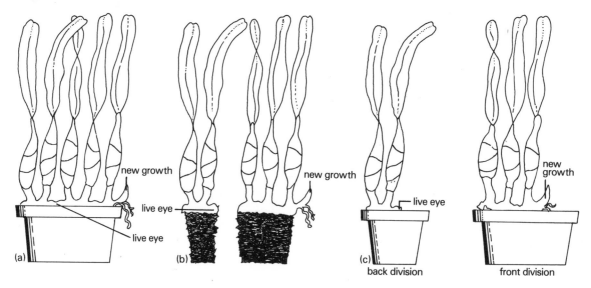

Reproduction by division. (a) Before division; (b) The divided plant; (c) The divided parts re-potted.

withered or dead, this pseudobulb will not make a new growth and the next one behind it must be examined. If this does have a live eye the knife is inserted between this and the pseudobulb in front of it. If this live eye is withered the one on the pseudobulb behind it must be inspected and so on. If none of the eyes on the pseudobulbs of the back division are live this division is useless and must be discarded.

If the eye on the very last and leafless pseudobulb does have a live eye there is a good chance of its growing and so this pseudobulb is removed by the knife. The front four pseudobulbs are potted up in the usual manner. The only pseudobulb remaining from the back four is planted in compost consisting mainly of sphagnum moss or it can be placed in a polythene bag, together with sphagnum, which is then closed tightly and suspended from a hook a yard or two from the glass in a warm or intermediate greenhouse. It will need no attention for some weeks, and the bud will commence to grow, and in due time will be advanced enough to be removed from the bag and potted in a small pot.

It matters not if the pseudobulb is leafless provided it has a live eye. Furthermore, in the case of a particularly fine variety, or of a rare plant, it would be possible to increase the stock of this plant by taking each pseudobulb having a live eye,

severing it from the others, and ending up with, for example eight pseudobulbs each with a growth, to become eight plants of flowering size in due time.

The newly repotted divisions, whether of plants divided into two or into eight pieces are kept in the shade for several weeks, and water is not given freely but the foliage is freshened daily with a mist sprayer.

A method of dividing cattleyas and similar plants and one which can be used practically at any time of the year is for a selected plant to be examined for a live eye, and for the sharp knife to cut the rhizome through partially, leaving both divisions of the plant in the pot. The eye starts in time to grow, the front division proceeding normally. When the time comes, in the spring, both parts can be potted up separately, and as there has been no disturbance to the roots, they are better than if they had been divided and repotted on the same day.

Paphiopedilums, not having pseudobulbs, but growths on a rhizome, are divided on the same system, but do not have the live eyes so readily seen in the cattleya. Paphiopedilums, more particularly the hybrids, make a growth or two each year and, as they require to be repotted every year, the time to divide is at repotting time. The species are different in this respect, and most can go two years before being repotted. The rhizome is tough in some cases, but the growths can be separated easily; frequently a knife is not necessary. This genus is one of the few which do not mind being repotted, indeed even when repotted in bud they are so resilient that they behave as though nothing out of the way had happened. After the plant has been divided, the original plant is in two pieces, a front piece with a flowered growth and a new growth and a back piece of a flowered growth.

The cymbidiums, with their sometimes enormous pseudobulbs are perhaps the easiest of all orchids to divide, and they are also perhaps the most divided of all orchid plants. The pseudobulbs vary in size and shape from the almost spherical to those which are almost oblong. The pseudobulbs without leaves are called back bulbs, and the arrangement of live eyes is slightly different from that of the cattleya. The live bud is at the base, like the cattleya's but there are a series of parallel rings circling the back bulb from the base to the apex, and the opposite bud is on the next ring up. This continues with the buds becoming fainter and more vestigial the further from the base they are. The rings on the cymbidium are similar to the leaf nodes on a dendrobium stem.

The bulbs are so close together that it is impractical to sever them like cattleya pseudobulbs while in the pot and so the plant has to be turned out. Cymbidium back bulbs are quick to establish themselves when given the right treatment and can be put in shallow trays bedded in sphagnum moss, kept constantly wet, on a plank of wood on warm pipes for a period of several weeks. When the growth is well developed they should be potted into individual pots. Polythene bags, too, are as efficaceous as when used with cattleyas. It is possible to find a cymbidium from a back bulb flowering after about three years.

The dendrobiums of the *D. nobile* type can be propagated in two ways, the first by separating the pseudobulbs, which are tall thin stems, in the same way as cattleyas and cymbidiums; however, the cane-like stem of the dendrobium often produces little plantlets either at the base of the stem or towards the top. These plantlets, or *keikis* (babies) have small leaves and a root system, and when large enough can be carefully separated from the main plant with a sharp knife and potted; in time they should mature into adult plants.

Vandas, renantheras and other Far Eastern genera are propagated in a crude but simple way which involves merely cutting off a foot or so of the leading growth at just below the point where there is a cluster of roots, and then potting up this piece. Aërides, etc. may be propagated in this way, but they, together with vandas frequently have small growths at the base, and these may be cut off carefully and potted.

There is one rule to apply when propagating by division, which is to divide only a plant in vigorous health and of large size, never a weak, sickly or small plant.

Hybridization

The first man-made orchid hybrid, *Calanthe* Dominyi, (*C. furcata × C. masuca*), raised, flowered and named in two years in 1856 by Veitch was the forerunner of the many thousands of hybrids of all kinds and from all parts of the world that are seen today. Increasingly vast numbers are sent for registration with the International Authority every year and the addenda to Sander's List of Orchid Hybrids are growing commensurately thicker with each five years' issue.

It is not surprising that a large proportion of the warmer-growing genera are raised in Hawaii and in Singapore and the intermediate ones in California, England and Australia. The flat *Vanda sanderana* (now placed into another taxonomic class and renamed *Euanthe sanderana*) has been responsible for a long line of hybrids, one of the first of which was *Vanda rothschildiana* (Chassaing, France, 1931); some of them interbred with other genera such as phalaenopsis, ascocenda and aërides.

The breeding, however, of intergeneric hybrids has surely reached a peak in the history of orchid hybridization with the granting of an Award of Merit by the Royal Horticultural Society's Orchid Committee in November, 1979 to *Hamelwellsara* Memoria Edmund Harcourt. This hybrid contains *Batemannia, Aganisia, Otostylis, Zygosepalum* and *Zygopetalum*. The number of different genera compares with those of a different sub-tribe in the make-up of *Goodaleara* which contains *Brassia, Cochlioda, Miltonia, Odontoglossum* and *Oncid-*

ium. All this has happened in only twelve decades of orchid hybridizing.

Pests and diseases

The tropical genera of the orchid family are not, when grown in artificial conditions, very susceptible to the inroads of pests, and what pests there are usually enter the orchid house through ventilators and doors in summer, and if the siting of the greenhouses is near trees, these provide a harbour for any number of insect pests. In the subtropics and other warm regions, an outside screen door, made of mosquito netting together with ventilators protected by the same material, do much to prevent the entry of insects and could usefully be employed more frequently in the temperate zones, during hot weather. Although bees can pollinate the larger orchids such as cattleyas and cymbidiums, they are generally regarded as pests in the orchid house and are best excluded.

There are, too, pests which attack species in the jungle: the cattleya fly which deposits its larvae in the stems and growing buds, and the dendrobium beetle which performs the same atrocity, but, due to the stringent import examination, these pests are no longer the menace they were.

To ensure the best possible conditions for the orchids, all weeds should be cleared from the surroundings of the orchid house, and, of course, inside too, and the cultural methods detailed previously observed.

Before DDT and BHC were proscribed by authorities in most orchid-growing countries, each was an efficient control for a variety of insect pests, such as thrips and aphids, but malathion is a splendid substitute and a spraying every now and then (three or four times during the summer) will keep the houses free. These insects together with mealy bugs, secrete a sweet substance called honeydew which is irresistible to ants which feed on it and transfer the insects from place to place in the greenhouse, hence the name for the insects of ant-cows. Ants are fairly simply eliminated from a greenhouse by the use of ant killer powder.

Hard scale, which appears mostly on cattleyas, but has also been reported on paphiopedilums and cymbidiums, requires a systemic insecticide, which is translocated through the orchid's system. This pest starts off by settling on a plant, usually on the underside of a leaf or in the membrane at the base of a pseudobulb in the case of a cattleya, and the hard shell gradually moves over the beak until this is in the centre of the shell, which renders the feeding insect impervious to anything but a scrubbing with a toothbrush or to a systemic insecticide.

Red spider mites are a scourge to cymbidiums and settle on the underside of leaves. Azobenzine 30 has been used for many years but pests can breed tolerant strains and a change of treatment is then essential. Malathion is a good control, as is also Murphy's systemic insecticide.

Slugs can be abolished for a time by distributing Fertosan over the plants, walls and the paths of the greenhouse a day after watering, and leaving it for a week or so. It does no harm to the plants and usually clears all evidence of slugs for about six months.

Springtails, (*Collembola orchesella*), are usually brought into the orchid-house in the sphagnum moss together with moss flies. BHC if obtainable will control them, and should be sprayed on after the plants have been watered. They emerge from the compost at this time. Malathion or lindane can also be used.

Mice can be a pest to cymbidiums during the pre-flowering period and gnaw through the buds to get at the pollen. Mouse poison placed throughout the house in small quantities is effective. The bait should be replenished daily until it appears not to have been touched; remove all unused bait at this juncture.

II Selection of Orchid Species

Paphiopedilum (Venus's slipper)

Tr. Cypripedieae Subtr. Paphiopedilinae

Etymology From *paphia* (Gr.) = additional name of Venus derived from the city of Paphos on Cyprus, and *pedilon* = slipper; called Venus's slipper because of the slipper-shaped lip.

Description This genus is the best known of all orchid genera which can surely be attributed to its common name. The characteristic slipper-shape of the lip is so fascinating and striking that everyone can easily recognize all examples of the Venus's slipper family. The genus *Paphiopedilum* consists of approximately 65 species; the native European and North American lady's slippers belong to the related genus *Cypripedium*. The natural habitat of paphiopedilums is limited to the region stretching from India through the Malayan Peninsula to New Guinea, the Solomon Islands and the Philippines. They are not found on the African, American and Australian continents. Most species are terrestrial, but there are also some lithophytic types. All species have evergreen, closely set leaf rosettes, from which develops a single flower stem with an individual flower or rarely, with two or more flowers. Its sympodial growth produces new pairs of leaves during the next growing season, causing a dense formation. However, it takes several years for the old leaves to wither. The paphiopedilums are mostly relatively easy to grow and their flowers give a lot of joy to their admirers for several weeks, even when cut and put in a vase. As regards the formation of the flower, in addition to the slipper-shaped lip, a further feature is that the two lateral sepals are joined together to form the synsepalum and usually remain relatively narrow so that they are hidden behind the lip. The dorsal sepal is usually large, and strikingly coloured. Orchid growers have already artificially produced thousands of hybrids which usually have large and particularly handsome flowers.

Cultivation Depending on their original habitat, some species require cool to intermediate conditions (usually plants having plain green leaves) and others (usually those with marbled leaves) prefer intermediate/warm or warm conditions. The paphiopediliums, being terrestrial orchids, do not like direct sunshine but require semi-shade. As they do not have any storage organs, they must not be subjected to a resting period. They can be watered every three to five days. Only after flowering should regular watering be somewhat restricted for a period of three to four weeks. However, at all times the compost must never be continuously saturated. Especially during spring and summer, sufficient humidity is necessary and, as is the case of all orchids, sufficient air circulation is advantageous so as to avoid stuffy conditions. Paphiopedilums are best planted in pots, the bottom quarter of which is filled with broken crocks to ensure adequate drainage. The compost consists of a mixture of osmunda fibre, sphagnum moss and some bark to which can be added a very small quantity of sand and leaf-mould. The size of the pots must be such that repotting will not be necessary for three to four years. In the case of *Paphiopedilum* hybrids, in contrast to species, repotting is done annually. When repotting, which is best carried out in spring, the old compost must be fully removed. The plant is placed in the centre of the pot and is firmly pressed down into the pot together with the compost. Until new roots are formed, the plants should preferably be mist sprayed and watering should take place very sparingly. Thereafter normal watering can be resumed. Strong plants can be divided and propagated in this way. *P. callosum* and *P. sukhakulii* are particularly suitable for window-sill culture.

Paphiopedilum callosum

Characteristics The 4–5 leaves grow to a length of 15 to 25 cm (6–8 in), are 4–5 cm (1½–2 in) wide and are variegated on the upper surface from light to dark green; underneath they are a uniform greyish green. The stem is dark violet and hairy, carries one to two flowers, and reaches a height of 25–35 cm (10–14 in). The flower, which lasts for eight to ten weeks, has a diameter of approximately 11 cm (4¼ in), possesses a roundish dorsal sepal, pointed towards the apex, with purple longitudinal stripes on the upper part changing to a greenish white with dark green longitudinal stripes on the lower part. The slightly S-shaped petals point downwards at an angle and have four to five small, round, brownish black and hairy calli (*callosum* = callous) on the upper edge. The petals are a light green at the base, changing to light violet

Paphiopedilum callosum (2/3 nat. size)

Paphiopedilum concolor

Characteristics The leaves are variegated dark green and grey green, approximately four in number, of a broad tongue-shape, and grow to a length of 10–15 cm (4–6 in) and to a width of approximately 4 cm ($1\frac{1}{2}$ in). The approximately 10 cm (4 in) tall flower stem has reddish hairs and carries one to (rarely) two flowers with a diameter of approximately 7 cm ($2\frac{3}{4}$ in). The flower shape is similar to the closely related *P. bellatulum*, apart from the pouch which is slightly more elongated. The petals curve slightly backwards at the apex. The colour of the flower is a uniform light yellow (*concolor* = uniformly coloured) with small violet/red dots.

Habitat Burma, Thailand to southern Vietnam.
Cultivation Intermediate to warm conditions.
Flowering season Spring or autumn.

Paphiopedilum hirsutissimum

Characteristics The strap-shaped, pointed and nearly uniform green leaves reach a length of 15–20 cm (6–8 in) and a width of approximately 2 cm ($\frac{3}{4}$ in). The stem grows to a height of approximately 15–20 cm (6–8 in) and carries a flower 10–12 cm (4–$4\frac{3}{4}$ in) in size. The dorsal sepal is of oval

towards the tip. The pouch is a strong purple brown merging to light green towards the tip.
Habitat Thailand, at altitudes of up to 750 m (2500 ft).
Cultivation Intermediate to warm conditions.
Flowering Season Usually autumn, winter.

Paphiopedilum concolor (× 1.1 nat. size)

Paphiopedilum hirsutissimum (2/3 nat. size)

Paphiopedilum spiceranum (nat. size)

shape and very heavily undulated around the edge; its colour is usually green with brownish violet spots. The side petals spread outwards, and are approximately 7 cm ($2\frac{3}{4}$ in) long and 2 cm ($\frac{3}{4}$ in) wide. They are recurved at the apex. The petal rim is very strongly undulated, particularly towards the base. The petals are at the base a basic green with dense brown violet spots with a light violet colouring towards the tip. Both petals and sepals are covered with coarse hairs (= *hirsutissimum*) around the edges. The slipper is green to red and usually covered with brownish violet dots.

Habitat India (Khasia Hills) at altitudes of approximately 1800 m (6000 ft).

Cultivation Cool to intermediate conditions.

Flowering season Spring.

Paphiopedilum spiceranum

Characteristics The leaves are strap-shaped and grow to a length of 15–25 cm (6–10 in) and a width of approximately 3 cm ($1\frac{1}{4}$ in). On the surface they are dark green and underneath towards the base they are speckled violet. The slim, dark red flower stem is 20–30 cm (8–12 in) long, is upright and carries one to (rarely) two flowers with a diameter of approximately 7 cm ($2\frac{3}{4}$ in), lasting for at least four weeks. The dorsal sepal is a broad oval, slightly reflexed at the edges. It is snow-white, changing into a green colour towards the base, which has a slight touch of violet, and which

also has a dark violet median stripe. The petals are tongue-shaped, spreading out and bent slightly forwards, with wavy fringes. Their colour has a touch of green and violet with fine violet spotting. The slipper is also green with more or less pronounced brownish violet veins. The staminode has a striking light violet edge.

Habitat India (Assam) at altitudes of 1000–2000 m (3330–6660 ft).

Cultivation Cool to intermediate conditions.

Flowering season Autumn.

Paphiopedilum sukhakulii

Characteristics This species was found by sheer accident as recently as 1964, and named after the Siamese orchid collector Sukhakul. The small, elliptical leaves, four to seven in number, reach a length of up to 25 cm (10 in) and a width of approximately 4–5 cm ($1\frac{1}{2}$–2 in). The surface is marbled dark green to light green and underneath they have fine red dots. The flower stem is dark brown and approximately 25 cm (10 in) long and carries one to (rarely) two flowers, 10–12 cm (4–$4\frac{3}{4}$ in) in diameter. The dorsal sepal is of an inverted heart-shape and is white with dense, dark-green longitudinal veins. The strap-shaped, pointed petals spread out horizontally and are approximately 6 cm ($2\frac{1}{2}$ in) long and 1.5 cm ($\frac{1}{2}$ in) wide. They are striped white to light green with dark green, and have numerous dark violet spots, their

Paphiopedilum sukhakulii (5/8 nat. size)

edges having dark hairs. The pouch is violet towards its opening and of a greenish colour towards its apex.

Habitat Thailand, at altitudes of up to 1000 m (3330 ft).

Cultivation Intermediate to warm conditions.

Flowering season Usually autumn.

Bulbophyllum

Tr. Epidendreae
Subtr. Bulbophyllinae

Etymology (Gr.) *bolbos* = bulb; *phyllon* = leaf.

Description This orchid genus possesses probably the largest number of species. Most recent estimates mention around 2000 *Bulbophyllum* species, growing mainly in all tropical and subtropical areas of the world (Africa, South America, Asia, Australia). Most species are small, but despite this they are not commonly found in the collections of orchid fanciers. A general description of this genus is very difficult in view of the multitude of species and their varying habit and differing flowers. Many cultivated species have single-leaved pseudobulbs which are arranged at set intervals on a creeping rhizome. The leaves are fleshy and differ in shape and size with the individual species. Sometimes flower spikes arise direct out of the pseudobulb or very close to its base, the flowers having an exotic appearance and

varying in number and size. In others, the flowers appear from a tall leaf, sometimes twisted into a spiral shape, and are arranged on both sides from the centre of the leaf. With many types the lip is connected with the base of the column through a hinge so that it can move fairly freely.

Cultivation It is only possible to give general and basic instructions for their care, as different cultural requirements apply for each species, even for each individual plant. The following basic instructions apply however for most *Bulbophyllum* species. Those species which grow in lower altitudes in the tropics require warm conditions, whereas those from higher mountain regions should be cared for under intermediate conditions. As the rhizome is creeping and is very heavily rooted, the plants should be cultivated on tree fern slabs, cork bark or in shallow bowls. Good drainage is important, as the roots do not tolerate stagnant conditions. A suitable compost is a mixture of sphagnum moss and osmunda fibre or chopped tree-fern. As some plants continue growing throughout the year, they require plenty of water and a high humidity. For deciduous *Bulbophyllum* species which experience very dry periods in their natural habitat (e.g. Himalaya region, Burma), the humidity should be reduced for a few weeks. However, species from tropical regions do not require this dry period. Many species grow best near glass, which must however be shaded from very strong sunlight, because the fleshy leaves and the pseudobulbs scorch easily. So as not to disturb the plants, they should be repotted as infrequently as possible, though exhausted compost must be replaced with fresh compost. No water should be allowed to remain on new growths and flower buds, as this could cause rotting.

Bulbophyllum cupreum

Characteristics In this species the rhizome and flower stem are very slim. The flowers are copper-coloured (= *cupreum*), unspotted and few. They are approximately 1.5 cm ($\frac{1}{2}$ in) in size; sometimes they do not open fully. The lips of the two species are only slightly different.

Habitat Burma, Philippines.

Cultivation Intermediate to warm conditions.

Flowering season Winter, spring.

(The species is illustrated overleaf.)

Bulbophyllum cupreum (× 1.7)

Bulbophyllum lobbii

Characteristics The yellow-green, egg-shaped
pseudobulbs grow from a strong rhizome at intervals of approximately 7 cm (2¾ in); they grow 3–5
cm (1¼–2 in) high. The solitary, leathery and
elongated leaves are approximately 20 cm (8 in)
long and 4.5 cm (1¾ in) wide. The waxlike and
longlasting flowers stand on an approximately 12
cm (4¾ in) long stem, which is arching due to
the weight of the flower. They open widely, have a
lovely scent, and are up to 10 cm (4 in) in size. The
sepals are approximately 6 cm (2½ in) long and
spreading, are lanceolate and tapering, and have a
pale yellow or reddish yellow colouring with red
spots on the under surface. The lateral sepals are
sickle-shaped. The petals are yellow, sometimes
striped red on the undersurface, grow to a length of
approximately 5 cm (2 in) and have the same basic
shape as the dorsal sepal, but are a little narrower.
The lip is only 2.5 cm (1 in) long, very flexible,
heart-shaped, pointed and revolute. It is yellow,
with more or less fine violet spotting, and has a small
orange mark at the base. The column is short, broad
and yellow with violet spots. This free-flowering
and often cultivated species was named after
Thomas Lobb, who discovered it in Java and
introduced it to England around 1846.

Habitat Thailand, Burma, Malayan Peninsula,
Sumatra, Java, Borneo.

Bulbophyllum lobbii (nat. size)

Cultivation Intermediate to warm conditions.
Flowering season Usually late spring, summer.

Bulbophyllum macranthum

Characteristics Whilst the general habit is similar to *B. lobbii*, it is overall smaller than that species. The single-leaved and egg-shaped pseudobulbs grow approximately 2.5 cm (1 in) high, and carry at the tip the tongue-shaped leaves, approximately 20 cm (8 in) long and approximately 5 cm (2 in) wide. The widely opening,

Bulbophyllum macranthum (× 2)

relatively large flowers (= *macranthum*), approximately 5 cm (2 in) in diameter, grow singly on short stems. The upper sepal and the petals are whitish, densely spotted with purple. The lateral bow-shaped sepals have a yellowish basic colour with purple spots on the under surface. Except for a short gap at the base they are fused together up to their tips. The small, flexible lip is yellowish and purple-red.

Habitat Malayan Peninsula, Indonesia to Borneo.
Cultivation Warm conditions.
Flowering season Spring.

Cirrhopetalum

Tr. Epidendreae Subtr. Bulbophyllinae
Etymology From Lat. *cirr(h)us* = curl; Gr. *petalon* = petal; referring to the curl-like twist in the lateral sepals.

Description The genus *Cirrhopetalum* comprises about fifty species and is closely related to bulbophyllums, and some botanists ascribe them to that genus. An epiphytic habit, and creeping rhizomes with single-leaf pseudobulbs, are common to both genera. *Cirrhopetalum* flowers are recognized by their umbellate arrangement and the greatly varying sepals. The upper, ovate sepal is smaller than the two lateral sepals, which are elongated and twisted and sometimes joined. The petals are relatively small and, with very few exceptions, possess tails at their tips. The lip is very small and, as with bulbophyllums, very flexible. Cirrhopetalums are found mainly in East Africa, Madagascar and throughout tropical Asia.

Cultivation Cirrhopetalums which are usually small in growth with relatively large flowers, require intermediate to warm conditions, depending on their original habitat. As epiphytes, they grow best on cork bark with a little compost, or on slabs of tree-fern. As many types do not store large reserves of nutrients, due to their small pseudobulbs, it is advisable to keep the water-free rest periods relatively short. They require sufficient light for the formation of flowers. Apart from this the cultivation is the same as for the related *Bulbophyllum* genus.

Cirrhopetalum guttulatum
syn. *Bulbophyllum umbellatum*
Characteristics The pseudobulbs are relatively widely spaced, are up to 5 cm (2in) long and of a narrow egg-shape, with one individual leathery, elongated leaf, which can reach a length of 18 cm (7 in). The flower stem is erect, slim and up to 20 cm (8 in) long and carries three to seven flowers 2.5–3 cm (1–1¼ in) long and arranged in a semicircle. The nearly round central sepal is approxi-

Cirrhopetalum guttulatum (× 3)

mately 1 cm ($\frac{3}{8}$ in) long and has five prominent veins. The lateral sepals are more oval, pointed and twice as long, their upper rim curved slightly inwards. The oval petals are only 0.5 cm ($\frac{1}{8}$ in) long. Petals and sepals are pale yellow and more or less evenly speckled purple (= *guttulatum*). The small, white and mobile lip is covered closely with dark violet spots and has a shallow groove. The short, yellow column has a horn-shaped appendage on both sides of the anthers.

Cirrhopetalum makoyanum (× 2)

Habitat Nepal, Himalaya area.
Cultivation Intermediate conditions.
Flowering season Autumn.

Cirrhopetalum makoyanum
Characteristics The pseudobulbs are approximately 3–4 cm ($1\frac{1}{4}$–$1\frac{1}{2}$ in) high and grow on the creeping rhizomes at intervals of 2–5 cm ($\frac{3}{4}$–2 in). At their apex is the tongue-shaped single leaf which narrows towards the base and grows to a length of 7–10 cm ($2\frac{3}{4}$–4 in) and a width of approximately 3 cm ($1\frac{1}{4}$ in). The violet flower stem is rather slim, 20–25 cm (8–10 in) long and carries approximately ten yellowish and finely red-violet spotted flowers in a fan-shaped to circular arrangement. The scented, very narrow flowers grow to 3 – 4 cm ($1\frac{1}{4}$–$1\frac{1}{2}$ in). The short dorsal sepal and the petals have yellowish hairs around the rim and threadlike tips. The narrow lateral sepals are joined for almost their entire length and give the flowers their distinctive appearance. The tongue-shaped lip is very small and inconspicuous.
Habitat Indochina, Singapore.
Cultivation Warm conditions.
Flowering season Winter.

Coelogyne
Tr. Epidendreae Subtr. Coelogyninae
Etymology From Gr. *koilos* = hollow; *gyne* = woman (*stigma*); referring to the hollowed stigma.
Description The genus *Coelogyne* is distributed over the monsoon areas of Asia, from India and Ceylon via Indonesia and the Philippines to the Fiji Islands and Samoa. This genus comprises approximately 125 species and is most strongly represented on the southern slopes of the Himalayas. The pseudobulbs, varying widely in shape and size in individual species, are connected by a strong rhizome. Depending on the species, they carry one to four broad, elliptic and usually folded leaves which vary widely in their size and texture. The upright, gracefully curved or pendulous inflorescences appear either at the base of the pseudobulbs or at their apices (sometimes between the leaves). The pleasantly scented flowers of the inflorescences flower either simultaneously or consecutively. There are also species having solitary flowers. The sepals are usually longer than the petals and are identical. The large, characteristic lip is usually tri-lobed, and the side lobes envelop the column more or less completely. The prominent two-part stigma is deeply inset, which gives the genus its name.
Cultivation Because of its rather wide distribution, there are species which require cool conditions and others which require intermediate or warm conditions. All species however require good drainage, whether they are planted in pots or in wooden baskets. As their growth is predominantly epiphytic, the roots will not tolerate stagnant conditions. The compost is a mixture of osmunda fibre or tree-fern fibres with a little sphagnum moss. The species can also be planted on slabs of tree-fern. Repotting should take place only when absolutely necessary, as they do not easily tolerate disturbance, and should be done after the rest period when new growth has commenced with new root shoots. In the case of the *Coelogyne* species from the tropics, which must be kept warm and which have continuous growth, the repotting time is very short. All species require rather bright but diffused light, as direct sunlight damages the leaves. The species requiring cool and intermediate conditions have a more or less pronounced rest period after the maturity of a new pseudobulb. During this time watering should be restricted. It is essential to observe a rest period at low temperatures so as to induce flowering.

Coelogyne cristata
Characteristics The densely arranged, nearly spherical pseudobulbs of yellowish green colour grow up to 6 cm ($2\frac{1}{2}$ in) long and shrink a little with age. The lanceolate pointed leaves are arranged in pairs and grow up to 30 cm (12 in) long and 3–5 cm ($1\frac{1}{4}$–2 in) wide. The flower stem grows erect from the base of the last pseudobulb, to a length of approximately 30 cm (12 in) and subsequently arches by the weight of the three to nine flowers at its head. The flowers are pleasantly scented, look like porcelain, and are beautifully waved and snow-white in colour, reaching 7–10 cm ($2\frac{3}{4}$–4 in) across. The small, elliptical, blunted petals and sepals bend forwards, but with their tips revolute. The lip protrudes and is tri-lobed with 5 golden yellow keels (comb-shaped = *cristata*) down the

Coelogyne cristata (3/4 nat. size)

centre. The rounded lateral lobes curl upwards and the tip of the central lobe backwards.

Habitat Himalaya area at altitudes of 1600–2500 m (5030–8030 ft).

Cultivation Cool conditions. This *Coelogyne* species has for many decades been a very popular orchid and is often described as the beginner's orchid. Its care is however not entirely without problems. For example, in autumn it requires a relatively low temperature (temperatures to nearly

Coelogyne ovalis (similar to *C. fimbriata*) (× 3.5)

freezing point do not cause any harm) so as to induce flowering. In summer it also requires a cool temperature, although higher temperatures are tolerated over a short period. This orchid is absolutely unsuitable for heated rooms.

Flowering season Winter, spring.

Coelogyne fimbriata
Characteristics   The   two-leaved   elliptical

pseudobulbs grow approximately 3 cm ($1\frac{1}{4}$ in) apart on a slim rhizome to a height of approximately 3 cm ($1\frac{1}{4}$ in). The rather thin and leathery, lanceolate leaves are 10–12 cm (4–$4\frac{3}{4}$ in) long and 2 cm ($\frac{3}{4}$ in) wide. The 5 cm (2 in) long stem carrying one to two flowers appears between the leaves at the top of the last pseudobulb. The 3 cm ($1\frac{1}{4}$ in) flowers can bloom repeatedly from one pseudobulb, have a musky scent and are rather long-lasting. The very narrow, reflexed petals and the long, pointed sepals are greenish yellow to brown. The tri-lobed lip is yellowish with red-brown stripes and veins. The short side lobes stand erect up to the yellow column. The nearly square central lobe has a finely fringed (=*fimbriata*) edge and two irregularly toothed keels which come together at the tip. This species is easily mistaken for the *C. fuliginosa* and *C. ovalis* which are similar in habit and flower. The flowering seasons are also no clear guide to recognition as they overlap from summer to winter. All three species grow under cool to intermediate conditions, though *C. ovalis* tends to prefer a more intermediate condition. In contrast to the other two species, the lip of *C. ovalis* is relatively pointed.

Habitat China to Thailand and Vietnam.
Flowering season Autumn.

Pleione

Tr. Epidendreae Subtr. Coelogyninae
Etymology Named after the mythological Pleione (Mother of the Pleiades).
Description The genus *Pleione* consists of about 15 species which, being mountain orchids, are usually to be found in the Himalaya region and in China at altitudes of 1000–3500 m (3300–11550 ft). They grow on the ground, on rocks, and also on trees. Their habit is fairly uniform. The pseudobulbs are not very large, closely arranged, usually covered with small warts, and are egg- to bottle-shaped; they carry comparatively long, creased and elliptical leaves which are deciduous. The pseudobulbs themselves do not survive for more than two years. The relatively large, attractive flowers appear singly at the base of the pseudobulbs together with the new shoots, i.e. during flowering the pleiones are leafless. The base of the lip is tubular in shape, from which extends the beautiful usually strongly fringed front lobe. The flower shape is very similar to that of *Cattleya* and also *Coelogyne*.

Cultivation Pleiones are best planted in bowls or pots which must be well drained. The best compost is a mixture in equal parts of loam, white sand, chopped sphagnum moss and chopped osmunda or tree-fern fibre. Some leaf mould can also be added. When planting, care must be taken that the short pseudobulbs are not buried in the compost and that the new growths are not covered with it. Water carefully after planting. Only after approximately six weeks, by which time there will be sufficient root formation, can regular and copious watering be resumed. The plants must be placed in a cool, humid, airy and shady place. Pleiones can also be planted in the garden. However, as they cannot withstand winter weather, they must be taken inside during the winter season. After the pseudobulbs have finished growing, the watering must be reduced so that they can ripen fully. In autumn, after the leaves have dropped, pleiones require a rest period during which the compost must be kept just moist enough so that the pseudobulbs do not shrivel. Only when buds appear can watering be resumed somewhat more freely to help development of the flowers. It is essential to repot yearly after flowering. When doing this, the pseudobulbs can be separated because during each vegetative period two new shoots are usually formed. This affords a good opportunity for propagation.

Pleione lagenaria
Characteristics The bottle-shaped (=*lagenaria*), brownish speckled and approximately 2.5 cm (1 in) long pseudobulbs have a central rounded protuberance. The lanceolate leaves grow to approximately 12–20 cm ($4\frac{3}{4}$–8 in) long. The flower stem carrying a single flower, reaches approximately 10 cm (4 in) and is densely enveloped with wrinkled sheaths. The 5 to 8 cm (2 to 3 in) flowers are slightly scented, with sepals and petals of similar lanceolate shape which spread out and are reflexed at the apex and have a tri-lobed lip. Sepals and petals are violet-pink in colour, often darker in the centre and at the tip. The side lobes of the lip, also coloured violet-pink, form a tube around the column. The roundish front lobe is slightly grooved at the tip and beautifully undulated

Pleione lagenaria (× 1.4)

around the margin. Its basic colour is white to violet-pink, yellow in the centre and white around the edge. In the centre it has dark violet longitudinal stripes and towards the edge dark-violet spots. Around the disc are five fringed keels.
Habitat India (Assam), Burma.
Flowering season Autumn.

Pleione maculata
Characteristics The bi-leaved pseudobulbs are approximately 2.5 cm (1 in) long, faintly speckled with brown and cylindrical, narrowing to a bottle-shape. The lanceolate, folded leaves reach a length of 15–20 cm (6–8 in) and a width of 3–4 cm ($1\frac{1}{4}$–$1\frac{1}{2}$ in). The short, sheathed flower stem carries one scented individual flower, approximately 6 – 8 cm

Pleione maculata (nat. size)

$(2\frac{1}{2} - 3$ in) in diameter. The sepals and petals are both lanceolate and both white, but the petals sometimes feature longitudinal violet lines. From the tri-lobed lip the two white lateral lobes form a closed tube, whereas the front lobe forms a nearly circular disk, slightly wavy around the edge. The front lobe has a broad white rim with radiating strong violet spots (*maculata* = spotted), the centre being predominantly golden yellow, otherwise white, with lengthwise violet lines and five toothed keels leading to the base of the lip.

Habitat Himalaya region.

Flowering season Autumn.

Dendrobium

Tr. Epidendreae Subtr. Dendrobiinae

Etymology From *dendron* (Gr.) = tree; *bios* (Gr.) = life; living on trees.

Description This genus is the second largest after *Bulbophyllum* with approximately 1600 known and defined species which are all epiphytic, as indicated by the name. This wealth of species gives rise to widely varying habit and flowers. The distribution stretches from the Himalayas to Australian regions and Pacific Islands and within this area they are found from the tropical warm sea altitudes to the cool mountain peaks. There are therefore species which are deciduous and those which are evergreen. The pseudobulbs of varying length are usually close together on the rhizome and are wedge-or spindle-shaped. The inflorescences can be either at the apex or at the edges of the pseudobulbs. They very often form gorgeous clusters of attractive flowers. A characteristic feature of all *Dendrobium* flowers is the 'chin' formation below the column, so that the lateral sepals usually stand at an angle. Petals and sepals look fairly similar, but the petals are usually broader than the sepals. The anther usually carries four pollinia. *Dendrobium* species are widely cultivated by orchid growers, as are the artificially produced hybrids which run into several hundreds. Dendrobiums are also offered as cut flowers by florists, in particular *D. phalaenopsis*.

Cultivation Most dendrobiums are among the relatively easily cultivated orchids. Depending on their natural habitat, there are types which require cool to intermediate conditions and others which require a lot of warmth for their growth. The 'cool' dendrobiums of the mountain regions (e.g. the best known type *D. nobile*), which do not always shed all their leaves, must be watered and syringed very freely during their growth period in the summer months. During this period they tolerate a lot of light, a high humidity and a great deal of warmth—occasionally even full sun. When the new shoots have stopped growing, the plants should be kept in a cooler place for one month and kept nearly completely dry. This induces the initiation of flower buds. Resiting in a warm atmosphere and with plentiful watering enables the flowers to develop properly. After the flower has opened, the growing period commences. The tropically 'warm' types, such as *D. phalaenopsis* and also the dendrobiums which require intermediate conditions, have no definite rest period. They need a sunny place and at all times sufficient water. Only during winter, when they are kept at somewhat lower temperatures, should watering be reduced. However, sufficient humidity is required at all times. All dendrobiums can be cultivated in pots and in wooden baskets (very good drainage!). Compost is made up of the usual mixture of osmunda fibre and sphagnum moss or similar ingredients. Species with pendulous pseudobulbs, as for example *D. loddigesii* must be cultivated in hanging pots or better still in wooden baskets. Species of small growth with creeping rhizomes, e.g. *D. aggregatum* can be cultivated on cork bark or tree-fern slabs. They are easily propagated by cuttings (amongst other methods) which are obtained through cutting off pseudobulbs and subsequently laying on or inserting in the compost. The young shoots appear at the nodes and their growth can be helped along by syringing. This also aids the formation of roots.

Dendrobium coelogyne

syn. *Epigeneium coelogyne*

Characteristics The two-leaved, approximately 6 cm ($2\frac{1}{2}$ in) long pseudobulbs, shaped like a squared-off ellipsoid, grow at fairly wide intervals on the scaly, long creeping rhizome. The tongue-shaped, rather leathery leaves grow approximately 10 cm (4 in). At the tip of the pseudobulbs the strongly scented, long-lasting and approximately

Dendrobium coelogyne (nat. size)

Dendrobium fimbriatum var. *oculatulum* (3/8 nat. size)

10 cm (4 in) single-flowers develop on short stems, which are similar to those of the genus *Coelogyne* (= *coelogyne*). The elongated, pointed sepals and the narrow, linear petals are about 5 cm (2 in) long, yellow on the reverse side, against a basic straw-coloured surface with uniform violet spotting. The petals are curved at the tip, whereas the lateral sepals are very strongly reflexed. The tri-lobed and dark violet-coloured lip consists of two small side lobes and an egg-shaped central lobe.

Habitat Burma, Thailand.
Cultivation Intermediate to warm conditions.
Flowering season Autumn.

Dendrobium fimbriatum

Characteristics The slim, stem-like pseudo-bulbs are arched slightly on account of their length of up to 1.5 m (5 ft) and thickened at the base. The lanceolate, pointed and dark green leaves grow to 10–15 cm (4–6 in) and last for about two years. The drooping, delicate flower clusters consist of seven to fifteen blooms, appear closely on top of the old, usually leafless pseudobulbs, and grow to approximately 20 cm (8 in) long. The flowers are approximately 7 cm (2¾ in) in diameter, and are of a brilliant orange-yellow colour. Both sepals and petals are broadly elliptical and approximately 3 cm (1¼ in) long. The petals are slightly toothed along the edge. The nearly circular lip is velvet-like and beautifully fringed (= *fimbriatum*). The variety *D. fimbriatum* var. *oculatum* is more often cultivated than the typical species and differs in having slightly larger flowers, petals which are usually not toothed, and two dark brown spots (*oculatum* = provided with eyes) on the disc of the lip which sometimes merge into each other.

Dendrobium nobile

Characteristics This widely cultivated and noble (= *nobile*) type varies considerably in measurements and colour of the flowers. The fleshy, cylindrical and multi-leaved pseudobulbs can grow to 45–60 cm (1½–2 ft) or even 90 cm (3 ft) high and develop grooves with aging. The lanceolate, up to 10 cm (4 in) long leaves are arranged alternately on the pseudobulb and drop off during the rest period after flowering. The one to three short-stemmed flowers are long-lasting, are wax-like and very heavily scented; they appear from the top nodes of the pseudobulb and reach 6–8 cm (2½–3 in) across. The narrow, elliptical sepals and petals are white to green at their base and change to a delicate rose-red or lilac towards their tip. The petals are slightly wavy. The cone-shaped lip is nearly round at its tip with a wavy margin. The colour of the lip gradually changes from a delicate rose-red or lilac rim into a white to green colouring with a deep purple blotch in the throat, which is sometimes encircled with a thin, yellow ring. Many hybrids have been produced from this species.

Dendrobium nobile (3/4 nat. size)

Habitat Himalaya area, South China to Taiwan and Vietnam.

Cultivation Cool to intermediate conditions.
Flowering season Late winter, spring.

Dendrobium phalaenopsis
Characteristics The long, slim and cylindrical pseudobulbs reach approximately 40–70 cm (16–28 in) high, from the upper part of which are developed the dark green leaves which last for

Dendrobium phalaenopsis (1/2 nat. size)

Dendrobium senile (3/4 nat. size)

several years. The leaves are leathery and grow to a length of approximately 10–15 cm (4–6 in). From the apices of the pseudobulbs arise the inflorescences, with three to fifteen beautiful flowers in sprays up to 50 cm (20 in) long, which arch with the weight of the flowers. The shape of the flowers is reminiscent of the *Phalaenopsis* genus (hence the name). The flowers vary in colour and have a diameter of approximately 8 cm (3 in). The petals are more than twice as wide as the elongated sepals, and are both either a nearly uniform red or have a white to pink basic colour which changes into a somewhat darker red towards the tip. The lip with its tongue-shaped, pointed front lobe is reddish to purple with more or less pronounced deep purple veins. The lip ends in a short spur. The species is commercially very important as it is eminently suitable for cutting because of its beautiful and long-lasting flowers.

Habitat New Guinea, Northern Australia.
Cultivation Warm conditions.
Flowering season Varying, usually spring; sometimes several times a year.

Dendrobium senile
Characteristics The cylindrical, pointed pseudobulbs usually reach a length of only 10 cm (4 in). They are covered with short white hairs,

particularly towards the top, which lends them a senile (= *senile*) appearance. At the apex of a pseudobulb are the two to three leathery, up to 7 cm (2¾ in) long leaves of inverted egg-shape, which are also covered with white hairs. The flowers issue, individually or in pairs, from the upper nodes of those pseudobulbs which have already shed their leaves. The long-lasting, wax-like flowers with a pleasant lemon scent are a brilliant yellow and grow to approximately 4–5 cm (1½–2 in). The sepals and petals are elongated and pointed. The petals are a little longer and broader than the sepals. The tri-lobed lip tapers to a point and has light green blotches on each side of the disc stretching from one side lobe to the other across the central lobe. The side lobes curve upwards as far as the yellow column.

Habitat Burma, Laos, Thailand.
Cultivation Intermediate conditions.
Flowering season Spring.

Brassavola
Tr. Epidendreae Subtr. Epidendrinae
Etymology Named after the Italian doctor and botanist Prof. Antonio Musa Brassovola (1500 to 1555).
Description The genus *Brassavola* comprises

approximately 15 species, most of which are epiphytic. They can be recognized from their habit; the thin, cylindrical stem-like pseudobulbs carry one or two fleshy, rush-like leaves with a nearly circular cross-section. The flowers are either single or in short clusters and issue from the joints between pseudobulb and leaf. Special characteristics of the flower are its five narrow sepals and petals and the unusually large lip which broadens out towards the front and envelops the column at the rear. *B. digbyana* is of particular value to the orchid grower, because crossing with *Cattleya* and *Laelia* species (*Brassocattleya* and *Brassolaeliocattleya* hybrids) has produced its strikingly beautiful lip in its progeny. The distribution of this genus stretches from Mexico and the Antilles to Brazil and Paraguay.

Cultivation *Brassavola* species like an intermediate to warm position with plenty of light. Some heavy leaves can even withstand full sunlight. During the growing period they require plenty of water. After the pseudobulbs have finished growing, watering should be restricted for a few weeks during the rather indefinite rest period. The cultivation is thus largely the same as for cattleyas and the same compost can be used as for cattleyas. *Brassavola* species are best planted in pots or baskets, where special attention must be paid to good drainage. Some have a pendulous habit and can be cultivated on bark or tree-fern. Propagation is by division of strong plants at the beginning of the growing season.

Brassavola flagellaris
Characteristics The very slim pseudobulbs ranging from 15 to (rarely) 25 cm (6–10 in) in length are bent in the shape of a whip (=*flàgellaris*), are circular and have a longitudinal groove. They end in a very sharp point; their length is 25 to (rarely) 40 cm (10–16 in). The loosely arranged inflorescence consists of three to eight flowers with a diameter of approximately 7 cm ($2\frac{3}{4}$ in). The pleasantly scented flowers last for about one month. The yellowish to greenish radiating sepals and petals are narrow, ending in a point and slightly reflexed. The white, elliptical lip encloses the yellowish column only at the base where it has a strong yellow throat.
Habitat Brazil
Flowering season Late spring.

Brassavola flagellaris (6/7 nat. size)

Brassavola nodosa

Characteristics The slim pseudobulbs have a circular cross-section and grow up to 15 cm (6 in) high. They each carry a single rather fleshy, lanceolate, tapering and erect leaf, which features a longitudinal groove. The leaves grow up to 30 cm (12 in) long and up to 1.5 cm ($\frac{1}{2}$ in) wide. The approximately 20 cm (8 in) long inflorescence contains a maximum of six flowers, 8–9 cm (3–3$\frac{1}{2}$ in) in diameter. The long-lasting flowers are scented, particularly at night. The narrow petals and sepals are a pale, greenish yellow. The lip is tubular at the base with a greenish colouring, but broadens towards the front into a heart-shape with a slightly wavy edge, white in colour with some purple spots around the opening.

Habitat From Mexico and the West Indies to Venezuela and Peru; at altitudes of up to 600 m (2000 ft) on rocks and trees.

Flowering season All year round, usually autumn to winter.

Cattleya

Tr. Epidendreae Subtr. Epidendrinae

Etymology This genus is named after the English orchid collector William Cattley (early 19th century).

Description This genus which consists of approximately forty natural species and some hybrids, is for most people the archetype of orchids. Cattleyas have long been counted amongst the best known and most sought-after orchids because of their beautiful, colourful and large flowers. Their value to the nurseryman has increased through the culture of specific hybrids and intergeneric hybrids (e.g. with *Brassavola, Laelia, Sophronitis*). It includes some of the most important orchids for nurseries specializing in cut flowers. *Cattleya* flowers are nowadays offered for sale by nearly every florist. All *Cattleya* species are epiphytes from the jungles of Central and South America. They have a strong root stock with usually erect, egg-shaped cylindrical pseudobulbs. At their apex there are one or two rather large, dark green, thick, leathery leaves. They can be divided into two groups according to the number of leaves, namely the single-leaved or *labiata* group, to which the *C. labiata* species belongs, with few, but relatively large flowers, and the twin-leaved group,

Brassavola nodosa (× 1.5)

which has many and somewhat smaller flowers. A sheath forms at the base of the leaves at the end of the growing period, and from this the inflorescence develops and emerges.

Cultivation Cattleyas, in particular the twin-leaved species, are relatively easy to care for if growth and rest periods are observed. Some species (e.g. *C. bowringiana, C. forbesii, C. loddigesii, C. skinneri*) can even be successfully cultivated on the window-sill. Most cattleyas require an intermediate position. During the growing period, which for many species commences in spring, they require plenty of water, although stagnant conditions should be avoided. As soon as the pseudobulbs have matured, watering should be reduced to avoid further growth of the plants and to induce formation of flowers. As soon as the buds can be seen in the sheath, watering should be increased. After flowering, the rest period commences, during which time the compost should be kept fairly dry and only a little watering approximately every two to four weeks is required. Cattleyas are known for their quest for light at all times. They should therefore be placed close to the glass (window or greenhouse) to ensure that the plants flower. As soon as new roots form after the rest period, repotting can be carried out, if necessary. The size of the pots must be such that repotting does not become necessary for another three years. New plants are easily propagated from the backbulbs which can be detached. A suitable compost is the usual mixture of osmunda fibre or chopped tree-fern with sphagnum moss and perhaps a little bark. A little gravel, charcoal or similar can also be added. Care must be taken that only the roots are covered by the compost, because the new growths must be able to develop freely and must not be kept moist. Dwarf species can also be cultivated on pieces of tree-fern.

Cattleya amethystoglossa

Characteristics The cylindrical, stem-like pseudobulbs, which develop grooves with age, reach a length of 70–100 cm (28–39 in), are enclosed by long-lasting, whitish sheaths and carry two leathery leaves which are broadly lanceolate, blunted and approximately 20 cm (8 in) long, 7–8 cm (2¾–3 in) wide. The long-stemmed, sometimes rather large inflorescence (30 cm (12 in) long

Cattleya amethystoglossa (1/3 nat. size)

and over) consists of four to ten flowers, about 10 cm (4 in) across. The coarse, wax-like and scented flowers have a narrow central sepal and broader lateral sepals and petals. Sepals and petals are white to pink with many dark violet spots. The trilobed lip consists of smaller whitish side lobes, the central lobe being crinkled and fringed around the edge and wedge-shaped at the base broadening into a wide kidneyshape towards its tip. The central lobe is white to cream-coloured in the centre towards the throat and amethyst (*amethystoglossa* = amethyst-tongued) towards the edge.

Habitat Brazil.

Flowering season Spring.

Cattleya bowringiana

Characteristics This species was named after Mr. J.B. Bowring (an amateur orchid grower from Datchet). The 30–50 cm (12–20 in) long, pillar-like pseudobulbs thicken to a spherical shape at their base and increase in diameter towards the top. The lanceolate leaves, approximately 15 cm (6 in) long and 6 cm (2½ in) wide issue horizontally from the end of the pseudobulb. The 15 cm (6 in) long inflorescence with five to ten (rarely more) flowers, 6–8 cm (2½–3 in) across and lasting for around two weeks, arises between the leaves. The pink to purple flowers are veined and glisten. The lanceolate, tapering sepals are narrower than the oval, rounded petals, both being slightly wavy.

Cattleya bowringiana (3/7 nat. size)

season is earlier (March to June).
Habitat Belize, Guatemala.
Flowering season Autumn.

Cattleya citrina
syn. *Encyclia citrina*

Characteristics This species differs from the other *Cattleya* species in various ways so that it has latterly also been considered as *Encyclia citrina*. As it grows on the underside of branches, it has a pendulous habit which is unusual for cattleyas. The egg-shaped, grey-green pseudobulbs, up to 7 cm (2¾ in) long and covered with whitish sheaths, are always above the two to three strap-shaped, tapering leaves, which are approximately 15 cm (6 in) long and 2.5 cm (1 in) wide. The pendulous leaves are grey-green and look as if covered with hoarfrost. A pleasantly scented flower, usually only around 8 cm (3 in) in size, develops on the stem which hangs downward and appears between the leaves. The flower is wax-like and lasts around two to three weeks. The elongated sepals and petals have a brilliant, lemon-yellow (= *citrina*) colouring. The large lip is golden yellow in its centre, fading towards the edge. It is attractively crinkled

The base of the lip encloses the column like a tube and is slightly indented at its tip. It is dark purple and thus slightly darker than the sepals and petals. Its throat is yellowish white with purple veins. From all appearances, including that of the flower, the species *Cattleya skinneri* cannot easily be distinguished from this species; only the flowering

Cattleya citrina (× 1.4)

Cattleya granulosa (nat. size)

around the margin. The yellowish column is not enclosed. In contrast with most *Cattleya* species, *C. citrina* requires a cool position. If this is provided in winter, then the plant is very prolific. **Habitat** Mexico; at altitudes of 2000–2500 m (6660–8320 ft).

Flowering season Summer.

Cattleya granulosa
Characteristics The slim, stem-like pseudo-bulbs grow approximately 40–60 cm (16–24 in) high. The rigidly leathery leaves are in pairs and

Cattleya schillerana (nat. size)

are lanceolate, blunted and about 15 cm (6 in) long. The short-stemmed inflorescence carries five to eight shiny, heavy, long-lasting and heavily scented flowers, 8–12 cm (3–4¾ in) across. The elongated, approximately 5 cm (2 in) long sepals and the somewhat broader petals are usually olive-green and have some dark red to brown spots; they are slightly undulated around their rim. The lip is strongly tri-lobed. The short, triangular side-lobes, whitish on the outside and yellowish to pink within, envelop the column. The projecting, fan-shaped central lobe is granular in the centre

(=*granulosa*) and finely fringed around the edge, its basic colour being white with pink spotting and yellow colouring with red markings towards the throat.

Habitat Guatemala, Brazil.

Flowering season Late summer, autumn.

Cattleya schillerana

Characteristics Named after the Hamburg orchid collector and alderman Schiller, this species is similar to *C. aclandiae* and requires warm conditions. It has slim, club-shaped pseudobulbs, 10–15 cm (4–6 in) long. The two dark green, fleshy leaves are elliptical and grow approximately 10 cm (4 in) in diameter. The short flower stem carries one or two flowers, about 10 cm (4in) in diameter, which are scented and long-lasting. Sepals and petals, undulated around their edges, are dark green to green-brown with dark brown blotches. The two side-lobes of the lip enclose the column. The central lobe broadens out to an inverted heart-shape and is purple with white veins, white to yellow around the edge and yellow towards the throat. The entire margin is slightly undulated and fringed.

Habitat Brazil.

Flowering season Summer.

Epidendrum

Tr. Epidendreae Subtr. Epidendrinae

Etymology From *epi* (Gr.) = upon; *dendron* = tree; living on trees.

Description This genus with more than 1000 species is one of the largest and is restricted to tropical America. They vary enormously with regard to habit and flowers. There are small and large species with or without conspicuous rhizomes. The number of leaves also varies considerably. Flowering is mostly in clusters, which usually appear at the apex of the pseudobulbs and form either panicles or beautiful clusters. A characteristic feature of *Epidendrum* species is the lip which is fused with the column. The flowers of some epidendrums are not twisted upwards (resupinated), so that the lip stands erect with these species.

Cultivation As with the related cattleyas, most *Epidendrum* species require intermediate conditions. During the growing period, which commences in spring, they require plenty of water and sufficient fresh, but not too warm air. They should be shaded a little as they do not readily tolerate direct sunlight. Sufficient humidity must be ensured. When the rest period commences in autumn after ripening of the new shoots, very little watering is required so as to induce flowering by temporarily drying out the plant. Most epidendrums can easily be cultivated in pots. The compost should be a well drained mixture of osmunda fibre or tree-fern fibre and sphagnum moss, to which can be added some beech leaves. The best repotting time is when growth commences with the formation of new roots. However, yearly repotting is not necessary. Climbing *Epidendrum* species can also be suitably cultivated on bark (e.g. cork) with a little compost or on tree fern slabs. The evergreen types with long stems prefer slightly warmer conditions. Their compost should never be completely dry during their rest period.

Epidendrum medusae

syn. *Nanodes medusae*

Epidendrum medusae (3/4 nat. size)

Characteristics Unlike many *Epidendrum* species, this species has dense foliage along the drooping stems which grow up to 20 cm (8 in). The thick and fleshy leaves, lanceolate and pointed in shape, cling to the stem for part of their 8 cm (3 in) (approximately) length; their colour is bluish green, sometimes tinged violet. The inflorescence carries one to three flowers, is short-stemmed and very compact. The strangely medusa-like (= *medusae*) flowers grow to a size of 7–8 cm (2¾–3 in). The oblong, approximately 4 cm (1½ in) long and slightly revolute sepals are yellow-green shot with red-brown. The petals are of the same colour and length, but only one third to one quarter as wide as the sepals. The approximately 6 cm (2½ in) large, kidney-shaped lip, fused with the column, is dark purple-brown with a very faint green centre. The edge of the lip has a very pronounced fringe.
Habitat Equador (in the Andes).
Flowering season Spring, summer.

Epidendrum polybulbon
syn. *Dinema polybulbon*

Characteristics Its many pseudobulbs (= *polybulbon*), approximately 2 cm (¾ in) in length, develop from the slim, creeping rhizome at 2–3 cm (¾–1¼ in) intervals. They are egg-shaped to ellipsoidal and carry at their apices two narrowish, elliptical leaves, which reach a length of only 3–6 cm (1¼–2½ in). Between the leaves appear singly (exceptionally in pairs) the long-lasting, scented and relatively large flowers on approximately 4 cm (1½ in) long stems. The rather narrow, pointed and spreading sepals and petals, nearly 2 cm (¾ in) in length, have a yellowish red to brownish red colouring. The round to inverted heartshaped lip, slightly wavy around the edge, is creamy white and yellowish at the base. The column is reddish on top; the anthers are also red.
Habitat Mexico, Guatemala, Cuba and Jamaica.
Flowering season Winter.

Epidendrum vitellinum
syn. *Encyclia vitellina*
Characteristics This species is frequently cultivated and is fascinating with its brilliant red

Epidendrum polybulbon (nat. size)

Epidendrum vitellinum (nat. size)

and tongue-shaped. The delicate inflorescence usually stands erect and reaches about 30–45 cm (12–18 in), depending on the number of flowers (ten to twenty). The long-lasting flowers are about 4 cm (1½ in) across. The spreading, elliptical but pointed sepals and petals shade from orange into a dark scarlet. The small, tongue-shaped, pendulous lip, which joins with the column only at the base, is yolk-of-egg yellow (= *vitellinum*).

Habitat Mexico, Guatemala.

Flowering season Autumn.

Isabelia

Tr. Epidendreae Subtr. Epidendrinae

Etymology Named in honour of the Brazilian princess Isabel de Alcantara (19th century).

Description This genus consists of one species only, which is epiphytic and found in the steaming, damp forests of Brazil. It is a dwarf plant with a strange appearance and delightful, relatively large flowers. It will give a lot of pleasure to connoisseurs of rare, small orchids.

Cultivation In its natural habitat, the *Isabelia* grows on small twigs and branches of trees in the continuously hazy, steaming forests. It has a

flowers. The egg-shaped, compressed pseudobulbs reach a length of 4–8 cm (1½–3 in) and usually bear two leaves. The 20–30 cm (8–12 in) long and approximately 5 cm (2 in) wide leaves are leathery

Isabelia virginalis (× 5.5)

creeping, sometimes long-branched rhizome. It is therefore advisable to cultivate it on bark or on flat slabs of tree-fern. Because of its small pseudobulbs it must never be allowed to dry out fully. On the other hand, the roots must also not be continuously saturated. It requires intermediate to warm conditions and, so far as light is concerned, should be placed in semi-shade.

Isabelia virginalis
Characteristics The densely arranged, egg-shaped, 7–10 mm ($\frac{1}{4}$–$\frac{3}{8}$ in) long, single-leafed pseudobulbs grow on the creeping rhizome and are covered with a network of fibres of brown to yellow, so that they look much larger than they actually are. From the apex of the pseudobulb arises an approximately 4–5 cm ($1\frac{1}{2}$–2 in) long, needle-like leaf (approximately 0.5 mm (under $\frac{1}{32}$ in) in diameter). The 10–12 mm ($\frac{3}{8}$–$\frac{1}{2}$ in) large, wax-like individual flower grows directly next to the leaf on such a short stem that it just peeps out of the network. The oval, tapering, spreading sepals are whitish with a slight violet tint. The narrow, oblong petals, rounded at the tip and turning slightly forwards, have a pure white colour. The broadly oval lip is also pure white. The approximately 2 mm ($\frac{1}{16}$ in) long column forms together with the anthers a small hood which is dark violet at the front.
Habitat Brazil.
Flowering season Late autumn, winter.

Laelia
Tr. Epidendreae Subtr. Epidendrinae
Etymology Named after the Roman general Gaius Laelius (2nd century BC).
Description This genus comprises approximately 60 species which are primarily epiphytic and are to be found in tropical America from Mexico to Brazil. They are closely related to the genus *Cattleya*. As they are often difficult to distinguish from cattleyas, their clear differentiation lies in the number of pollinia: laelias have eight (arranged in two sets of four), cattleyas have only four. *Laelia* species differ widely in habit, some having short, closely arranged pseudobulbs, others long ones like the cattleyas. The large flowers are attractive, usually with striking, tri-lobed lips, with side lobes enclosing the column in the same way as cattleyas. Hybridizers like laelias for crossing, in particular with cattleyas, resulting in the very beautiful laeliocattleyas.
Cultivation Similar to that for the *Cattleya* genus; most *Laelia* species are kept under intermediate conditions. Room culture is possible if humidity is sufficient. During the growth period sufficient watering is necessary, and also some syringing. To induce flowering, watering should be rationed, otherwise vegetative growth can occur without the formation of flowers. Many species, particularly those from Brazil, require full sunshine for the formation of flowers. For other species, a light, but slightly shady place is sufficient. During the flowering season normal watering can be resumed. A rest period follows after flowering, during which watering should be restricted (about every two weeks). No exacting demands are made with regard to humidity, although it should be endeavoured to obtain a relative humidity of between 60 and 70%.

Laelia species can be cultivated either in pots with good drainage or in meshed baskets. The compost should be the same mixture as for cattleyas, i.e. mainly osmunda fibre and sphagnum moss and perhaps some bark. It is important that the compost dries fully out between watering. With the commencement of the growing period, which can be recognized by the starting of new roots, repotting can take place, if necessary. This should however be done only about once in three years. New plants can be cultivated from separated backbulbs.

Laelia anceps
Characteristics The single-leaved pseudobulbs are of an elongated egg-shape and compressed. They grow 5–7 cm (2–$2\frac{3}{4}$ in) high. The leathery lanceolate, pointed leaves reach approximately 15 cm (6 in). The slim, 50–70 cm (20–28 in) long flower stem, growing out of the apex of the pseudobulb, is erect or bends slightly through the weight of the two to five loosely arranged flowers. The viscous flower stem is typically two-bladed ($=$ *anceps*) and has small leaves. The flowers are 8–10 cm (3–4 in) across and have a lighter or darker violet-pink colouring. The lanceolate, pointed sepals are 5–6 cm (2–$2\frac{1}{2}$ in) long

Laelia anceps (nat. size)

and approximately 1.5 cm ($\frac{1}{2}$ in) wide, whereas the elliptical and pointed petals have the same length, but are twice as wide as the sepals. The tri-lobed lip encloses the column with its side lobes. The dark purple central lobe is of elongated egg-shape, sometimes pointed and white in its centre with three yellow ridges. The throat is yellow with purple veins.

Habitat Mexico. Honduras; at altitudes of between 1000–2000 m (3330–6660 ft).

Flowering season Winter.

Laelia harpophylla

Characteristics The slim, cylindrical pseudobulbs, closely arranged in clusters, are erect and grow 15–30 cm (6–12 in) long. At their apices grow individually, in the shape of a narrow tongue, the leathery, pointed and hooklike leaves (= *harpophylla*), 15–20 cm (6–8 in) long and approximately 3 cm (1$\frac{1}{4}$ in) wide. The inflorescences, with four to seven flowers, which remain shorter than the leaves, consist of 5–8 cm (2–3 in) long-lasting flowers of a striking vermilion, with light yellow at the centre of the lip. The spreading, lanceolate

sepals and petals look similar to each other and are approximately 4 cm (1$\frac{1}{2}$ in) long. The strongly tri-lobed lip consists of two triangular side lobes which surround the bent column and a long, partly reflexed central lobe, which is heavily undulated around the edge and which carries two ridges on the disc.

Habitat Brazil.

Flowering season Winter.

Laelia purpurata

Characteristics The spindle- to wedge-shaped, slim pseudobulbs reach up to 60 cm (24 in) in length and carry one leathery, tongue-shaped leaf, 30–40 cm (12–16 in) long. The three- to seven-flowered inflorescence develops at the apex of the pseudobulbs in a sheath. The flowers measure 15–18 cm (6–7 in), being the largest of this genus, and sit on a short stem. The lanceolate sepals are slightly reflexed at the tip and at the base. The petals are twice as wide, elongated, egg-shaped and undulating along the edge. Sepals and petals are whitish with a slight or more pronounced touch of light pink. The tri-lobed tubular lip encloses the

Laelia harpophylla (× 1.4)

Laelia purpurata (2/3 nat. size)

column. The central lobe extends downwards. It is white at the tip and shows a strong purple (= *purpurata*) towards the throat. The throat itself is yellowish with violet veins.

Habitat South Brazil.

Flowering season Spring, summer.

Leptotes

Tr. Epidendreae Subtr. Epidendrinae

Etymology From *leptotes* (Gr) = delicacy; referring to its delicate and dainty habit.

Description There are approximately six epiphytic species, all small in growth and possessing relatively large and attractive flowers. Their origin is Brazil and Paraguay. Their fleshy leaves, which have a nearly circular cross-section and grow singly on stunted, stem-like pseudobulbs, give them the appearance of dwarf brassavolas. The inflorescence develops from the leaf axil, bearing very few flowers, which consists of spreading petals and sepals, similar to each other, and a tri-lobed lip, the small side lobes of which are vertical alongside the short column.

Cultivation The *Leptotes* species are relatively easy to grow and to flower, requiring intermediate conditions as in their natural mountain forest habitat. They need slight shade, fresh circulating air and a rather high humidity. They thrive on tree-bark with a little compost, and they can also be planted in small pots with good drainage in a compost of osmunda or tree-fern fibre with just a little sphagnum moss. During the growing season watering or immersion should only be done when the compost or the tree-fern is dry, so that new shoots do not rot. When the growths have grown to their full size, watering should be somewhat restricted to induce flowering and so as to avoid continued vegetative growth. As soon as the flower bud shows in the leaf axil, normal watering can be resumed. During the rest period after flowering, water should be given sparingly. *Leptotes* species like to be hung up in the garden or on the balcony in a shady position during summer.

Leptotes bicolor

Characteristics The stem-like, approximately 2 cm ($\frac{3}{4}$ in) long pseudobulbs bear a fleshy, pointed leaf with a central groove on the surface, sometimes bent into a sickle-shape, approximately 5–10

Leptotes bicolor (× 1.5)

cm (2–4 in) long and 6–8 mm ($\frac{7}{32}$–$\frac{5}{16}$ in) in diameter. The flowers of the short-stemmed inflorescence of two to six scented flowers, approximately 4 cm (1$\frac{1}{2}$ in) across, bloom one after another and last for approximately four to six weeks. The tongue-shaped sepals and petals, which curl forwards at their tips, are fleshy in texture and snow-white in colour. The tri-lobed lip consists of a tongue-shaped, pointed, approximately 1.5 cm ($\frac{1}{2}$ in) front lobe of a strong pink-violet colour, and two small, ear-shaped vertical white side lobes. The column stands free and is olive green.
Habitat Brazil, Paraguay.
Flowering season Usually winter, spring.

Sophronitis

Tr. Epidendreae Subtr. Epidendrinae
Etymology From *sophron* (Gr.) = chaste, modest, shy; referring to the hidden anthers and the rather small growth of the plants.
Description This genus consists of seven diminutive, epiphytic and decorative species which all originate from the Organ Mountains of Brazil. In relation to the size of the plant they have large, brilliant red or violet flowers which make them favourites with orchid raisers. On the creeping rhizome are small, flat to round pseudobulbs which carry at the apex a rather fleshy single leaf. The inflorescences appear from the apices of the pseudobulbs, either as single flowers or are multi-florous. The sepals and petals are star-shaped, and are rather similar to each other. The undivided lip encloses the short column.
Cultivation As all *Sophronitis* species are found at altitudes of approximately 1500 m (5000 ft), they are best grown under intermediate conditions, although they can well withstand cold conditions for short periods. They can be kept either in small pots with good drainage or on pieces of bark with a little compost or on tree-fern slabs. Compost is as for epiphytes, namely a mixture of osmunda or tree-fern fibre with chopped sphagnum moss. Most *Sophronitis* species have no marked rest period, thus requiring regular and plentiful watering. It is however important for healthy root conditions that the water drains off and that there is no stagnation. Being mountain orchids, they furthermore require a relatively high humidity

with good air circulation and a semi-shady place. *S. cernua* can however withstand a little sun and should have a very short rest period for the formation of its pseudobulbs. Unfortunately it is difficult to maintain *Sophronitis* species in a good condition for a period of years.

Sophronitis coccinea
syn. *Sophronitis grandiflora, S. rosea*
Characteristics The spindle-like to cylindrically oval pseudobulbs stand closely together, grow 2.5–3.5 cm (1–1$\frac{3}{8}$ in) high and carry a short-stemmed, leathery, elliptical and dark-green single leaf, 6–8 cm (2$\frac{1}{2}$–3 in) long and approximately 2 cm ($\frac{3}{4}$ in) wide. The 5–7 cm (2–2$\frac{3}{4}$ in) flowers usually grow singly and sit on a short stem which springs from the tip of the pseudobulbs. The colour of the flower is usually a brilliant scarlet (= *coccinea*), more rarely a violet pink. The sepals are the shape of a flattened oval and approximately 3 cm (1$\frac{1}{4}$ in) long. The petals are twice as wide, spread out horizontally, are oval to nearly rhomboidal in shape, and reach a length of approximately 4 cm (1$\frac{1}{2}$ in). The faintly tri-lobed, approximately 2.5 cm (1 in) lip encloses the column, forming a small cone. At its base the lip is a reddish yellow with scarlet veins. This *Sophronitis* is not only the best-known species, but also the most cultivated and the most beautiful, so that it is not surprising that it is used for hybridization. The best-known hybrids are those crossed with *Cattleya* and *Laelia* species which are then named *Sophrocattleya* or *Sophrolaelia* respectively.
Habitat Brazil.
Flowering season Autumn, winter.

Sophronitis violacea
syn. *Sophronitella violacea*
Characteristics The ellipsoidal pseudobulbs stand erect and closely together, have longitudinal grooves and grow 1.5–3 cm ($\frac{1}{2}$–1$\frac{1}{4}$ in) high. The narrow lanceolate, leathery leaves stand singly and reach 4–7 cm (1$\frac{1}{2}$–2$\frac{3}{4}$ in) long. The short flower stems carry one or two flowers, 3–4 cm (1$\frac{1}{4}$–1$\frac{1}{2}$ in) in diameter, which last approximately two weeks. Their colour is a strong violet (= *violacea*) which sometimes shades towards the centre of the flower into a pink-violet. The sepals and petals are starshaped, the petals being slightly the shorter,

Sophronitis coccinea (× 1.5)

Sophronitis violacea (× 2.5)

and both being of a pointed oval shape. The oval lip is as long as the petals. The anthers have a dark violet colour.

Habitat Brazil.

Flowering season Winter.

Masdevallia

Tr. Epidendreae Subtr. Pleurothallidinae

Eytmology Named after the Spanish doctor and botanist Jose Masdevall (18th century).

Description The approximately 300 species of the genus *Masdevallia* are so characteristic and uniform in their flower structure that they are easily recognized. They are usually epiphytes, although some are terrestrial and some lithophytes. The distribution area stretches from Mexico to Brazil and Bolivia, but nearly 75% of all species are found in the foggy forests of the Colombian Andes. Masdevallias do not have pseudobulbs. The leathery, shiny green leaves narrow towards their base and grow densely from the plant's creeping rhizome. The flower stem develops in the leaf axil and bears usually only one, but in some cases up to eight flowers. The flower is dominated by the triangularly arranged, relatively large sepals which fuse together at the base and usually end in long tails. The petals are rather stunted and barely visible. The lip is also very small.

Cultivation Depending on their habitat, most *Masdevallia* species must be kept under cool, shady conditions and at a high humidity. They have no rest period so that sufficient and constant moisture should be ensured at all times, although watering can be reduced a little during winter. They furthermore love plenty of fresh and circulating air. They are best planted in small pots with very good drainage, so as to avoid stagnation. Compost can be the usual mixture for epiphytic orchids, i.e. a mixture of osmunda fibre and sphagnum to which can be added a little bark or polystyrene shavings. Some species, as for example *M. chimaera*, are better cultivated in wooden baskets in view of their pendulous flowers. In many species the flower stems should not be cut immediately after the first bloom, as it is possible

Masdevallia caloptera (× 1.8)

Masdevallia caudata (2/3 nat. size)

for flowers to develop again during the next flowering season.

Masdevallia caloptera
Characteristics The 6–8 cm ($2\frac{1}{2}$–3 in) long and 1.5–2.5 cm ($\frac{1}{2}$–1 in) wide leaves grow closely together from a short rhizome and stand on a stem up to 1.5 cm ($\frac{1}{2}$ in) long. They are leathery, elongated and blunted at the tip. The stem carrying two to six flowers grows to 12–15 cm ($4\frac{3}{4}$–6 in). The oval central sepal is shaped like a cup, slightly toothed around the edge and its overall length is 1.5–2 cm ($\frac{1}{2}$–$\frac{3}{4}$ in) including the 5 mm ($\frac{3}{16}$ in) long and 1 mm ($\frac{1}{32}$ in) wide, greenish yellow lobe. All sepals are white with strong violet spots. The 4 mm ($\frac{5}{32}$ in) long, white petals are hidden beneath the central sepal. The tongue-shaped, 4 mm ($\frac{5}{32}$ in) long lip forms beneath the central sepal protruding upwards at an angle and is a pale to strong violet. The name *caloptera* means beautifully winged.
Habitat Peru, Colombia; at altitudes of approximately 2200 to 2800 m (7320 to 9320 ft).
Flowering season Winter (December, January).

Masdevallia caudata
Characteristics The leathery leaves have an elongated, spatula-like shape, are 5–7 cm (2–$2\frac{1}{4}$ in) long and are borne on slim stalks of similar length. The erect flower stem is 15 cm (6 in) high and carries one long-tailed (= *caudata*) single flower with an overall length of approximately 16 cm ($6\frac{3}{8}$ in). The concave central sepal is yellowish to ochre coloured, with a reddish tint towards its edge and has seven red inner longitudinal veins. The egg-shaped, lateral sepals are spotted violet and white and spread outwards at an angle. All sepals end in yellowish, thread-like tails, approximately 6 cm ($2\frac{1}{2}$ in) long, which radiate outwards. The very small, elongated petals are white. The small, tongue-shaped lip is curved forwards and densely covered with pink-violet spots.
Habitat Colombia; at altitudes of approximately 2500 m (8320 ft).
Flowering season Late autumn, winter.

Masdevallia edwallii
syn. *Trigonanthe edwallii*
Characteristics Named after the botanist and orchid collector Edwall, this dainty species has leathery leaves which broaden upwards and then end in a point, measuring with the short stem approximately 6–8 cm ($2\frac{1}{2}$–3 in) long and approximately 1 cm ($\frac{3}{8}$ in) wide. The large, attractive single flower is borne on a short stem of approximately 2 cm ($\frac{3}{4}$ in). The sepals are joined together at the base for about 3 mm ($\frac{1}{8}$ in) and are

Masdevallia edwallii (× 3)

yellow in colour with red-brown spots. The egg-shaped to triangular, short-lobed central sepal projects upwards and slightly forwards, being approximately 1 cm ($\frac{3}{8}$ in) long. The oval lateral sepals, tapering into tails, are 6 – 7 mm ($\frac{7}{32}-\frac{1}{4}$ in) wide at their base and overall 1.5–2 cm ($\frac{1}{2}-\frac{3}{4}$ in) long, half of this length being accounted for by the tails. The small, nearly square to trapeziform petals are approximately 3 mm ($\frac{1}{8}$ in) long and at their tip 4 mm ($\frac{5}{32}$ in) wide with weak toothing around the edge. The tongue-shaped, reddish brown lip is only a few millimetres long.

Habitat Brazil (Minas Gerais to Parana).
Flowering season Winter.

Masdevallia tovarensis

Characteristics The leathery, elliptical to spatula-shaped leaves, which are slightly toothed at their apices, grow to a length of 12–15 cm ($4\frac{3}{4}$–6 in). The triangular flower stems are approximately 15–18 cm (6–7 in) long and carry two to four widely opened wax-like and fairly long-lasting flowers, which are about 3 cm ($1\frac{1}{4}$ in) wide and 9 cm ($3\frac{1}{2}$ in) long between the tail points. The whitish flowers are transparent with some snow-white longitudinal veins. The lateral sepals are fused together and form a broadly oval surface which extends downwards into two needle-like pale yellow tails, approximately 3 cm ($1\frac{1}{4}$ in) long. The

central sepal consists mainly of the 3–4 cm ($1\frac{1}{4}-1\frac{1}{2}$ in) long and needle-shaped tail which is vertical. The small petals and the small lip are also white.

Habitat Venezuela, in the Tovar (= *tovarensis*) region at an altitude of approximately 2000 m (6660 ft).

Masdevallia tovarensis (1/2 nat. size)

Masdevallia veitchiana (3/4 nat. size)

Flowering season Late autumn, winter.

Masdevallia veitchiana
Characteristics This species introduced to England in 1867 by Veitch (= *veitchiana*) has elongated, inverted lanceolate leaves, 15–20 cm (6–8 in) long. The 30–45 cm (12–15 in) long flower stem carries one or two plain-coloured, brilliant vermilion flowers with an overall length of 12–15 cm ($4\frac{3}{4}$–6 in) and a width of 4–5 cm ($1\frac{1}{2}$–2 in). The sepals fuse together at the base and form a short funnel, from which the triangular free part of the central sepal extends upwards, tapering to a slim tail and the two lateral short-tailed sepals extend downwards, growing together for up to two thirds of their length. The small petals, sitting inside the sepal funnel, and the small lip are all white.
Habitat Peru; at altitudes of 3500–4000 m (11 660–13 320 ft) on rocks.
Flowering season Spring.

Pleurothallis

Tr. Epidendreae Subtr. Pleurothallidinae
Etymology From *pleuron* (Gr.) = rib, side; *thallo* (Gr.) = bloom; referring to the floral segments relative to the axis.
Description This genus is distributed in tropical America, where there is a proliferation of species. Their number is estimated at nearly 1000, to be found from south Florida via Mexico and the Antilles to Argentina and Bolivia, the largest concentration being between Mexico and Brazil. *Pleurothallis* species are usually epiphytes and have a widely varying appearance. There are small, moss-like species, the size of a thimble and elegant shrubs growing to 0.5 m (20 in) and more. None of the species has pseudobulbs. A thickish stem carries a simple leaf which varies greatly from one species to another. The inflorescence usually appears in the leaf axils. The flowers, sometimes small, sometimes large, are very interesting and appear singly or in multifloral spikes. The sepals are strikingly dominant, with the lateral sepals usually fused together. The petals and in particular the lip are considerably smaller and less conspicuous than the sepals. Although there are some quite attractive species with beautiful flowers, the *Pleurothallis* genus is not very commonly represented in private orchid collections. Unfortunately only very few species are offered commercially.
Cultivation Being epiphytic orchids, *Pleurothallis* species can be grown in small pots with good drainage and on tree-fern slabs. Compost is either osmunda or tree-fern fibre, perhaps with a little chopped sphagnum moss. These pseudobulbless orchids require no rest period so that they must be always kept evenly moist, i.e. the roots must never be allowed to dry out. However, stagnant conditions must be avoided. Sufficient humidity (about 70% relative humidity) and a good air circulation are required. Most *Pleurothallis* species grow under intermediate conditions, although some are also found in cooler or warmer regions, depending on the altitude at which they are found in the mountains. They should be placed in semi-shade so that the fleshy leaves are not scorched by the sun's rays. Repotting should be carried out only rarely (about every four years), as the plants

Pleurothallis sonderana (×2)

are sensitive to change . If a pot becomes too small because of the all-round growth of new shoots, a strong plant can be propagated by division. All in all, *Pleurothallis* are relatively easily cared for.

Pleurothallis sonderana

Characteristics The thin, round and closely growing stems, 3–5 cm ($1\frac{1}{2}$–2 in) long and 1 mm ($\frac{1}{32}$ in) in diameter, are surrounded at the base with paper-like sheaths. They carry a single, thick, fleshy leaf with a cross-section of approximately three-quarters of a circle (3–4 mm ($\frac{1}{8}$–$\frac{5}{32}$ in) in diameter) and a length of 2 – 2.5 cm ($\frac{3}{4}$– 1 in). From the base of the leaf, and on its very strongly grooved surface, the inflorescence of three to six flowers develops and just protrudes beyond the leaf on its 0.5 mm (less than $\frac{1}{32}$ in) stem. The flowers, barely 1 cm ($\frac{3}{8}$ in) in size, uniformly yellow to orange-coloured, last around four to five weeks. A small plant can produce more than 100 flowers

and can thus be entirely smothered in yellow. The small, elliptical sepals in the shape of a beak, form the central point, with the lateral sepals fused almost as far as their tips. The similar-looking petals are only half as long as the sepals; the small lip is shorter still. The short column carries at its apex brilliant yellow pollinia.

Habitat Brazil.

Flowering season Summer, autumn.

Pleurothallis strupifolia

Characteristics The slim, round and approximately 15 cm (6 in) long stem is for around 2 cm ($\frac{3}{4}$ in) of its length enclosed by a sheath and carries a strap-shaped leaf (= *strupifolia*), 10–12 cm (4–4$\frac{3}{4}$ in) long. The flower spikes have tightly compressed blooms, fifteen to twenty in number, and are only half as long as the leaves. The 1–1.5 cm ($\frac{3}{8}$–$\frac{1}{2}$ in) large flowers are red with dark red spots. The lateral sepals, which dominate the bloom, are

Pleurothallis strupifolia (× 3)

joined together for approximately half their length. The petals and the lip of this plant are insignificant.

Habitat Mexico to Brazil.

Flowering season Summer.

Restrepia

Tr. Epidendreae Subtr. Pleurothallidinae

Etymology Named after the Colombian naturalist Jose E. Restrepo.

Description This genus comprises approxi-

Restrepia guttulata (× 3)

mately 35 species and is closely related to the *Pleurothallis* genus, with which it shares a similar appearance, but differs in having four pollinia. Many types have very narrow, antenna-like petals. However, this is not characteristic of all species.

Restrepias have no pseudobulbs. The leaf stalks, which are surrounded by a small sheath, grow from the rhizome usually in clusters, and carry single leaves at their apices. The flower stem develops from the leaf stalk shortly below the leaf base, is surrounded by a sheath and is covered by a bizarre solitary flower. As the leaves are usually somewhat twisted, the flowers appear on the underside of the leaf. The lateral sepals are normally joined together and noticeably larger than the tongue-shaped lip, which almost rests on these sepals. The distribution area for *Restrepia* species stretches from Mexico via Venezuela to North Argentina, where it is found only in higher mountain regions.

Cultivation Depending on their habitat, restrepias must be cultivated under cool conditions, which is not always easily achieved during summer. In any case, they always require a sufficiently moist compost and humidity so that the pseudobulbless plants do not dry out. They furthermore like good ventilation and a place in the semi-shade. During the growing period from spring onwards, watering should be carried out freely, whereas in winter only so much water should be given to ensure that the compost does not dry out. *Restrepia* species are best planted in small pots with good drainage. The compost consists of the usual mixture of osmunda fibre and sphagnum moss. Repotting is every three to four years; propagation is possible through division of strong plants. Sometimes vegetative growths will form instead of flowers.

Restrepia guttulata
syn. *Restrepia maculata*
Characteristics The tough, elliptical individual leaves, 6–8 cm (2½–3 in) long and 3 cm (1¼ in) wide, are borne on stems up to 11 cm (4½ in) long, which are enclosed with whitish, speckled and paperlike sheaths. In size, this species is similar to *R. antennifera*, but the flower stems, being approximately 7 cm (2¾ in) in length, are somewhat longer. The sepals are about 2.5 cm (1 in) long; the antennae-shaped petals reach only half this length. The central sepal, projecting upwards, is approximately 3 mm (⅛ in) wide, the lateral sepals being joined together and about 1 cm (⅜ in) wide. The colouring of the entire flower is similar to *R. elegans*, i.e. the lateral sepals and the lips are orange yellow with small dark red spots (=*guttulata*) arranged in rows lengthwise. The upper part of the lip is covered with small warts.
Habitat Venezuela, Colombia, Ecuador; at altitudes of 1300 to 2300 m (4330 to 7660 ft).
Flowering season Winter.

Cymbidium

Tr. Maxillarieae Subtr. Cymbidiinae
Etymology From *kymbos* (Gr.) = boat; referring to the boat-shaped recess in the lip.
Description This very popular genus comprises about 70 species which can be terrestrial, lithophytic or epiphytic. The pseudobulbs are usually oval, carrying rather long, tough and strap-shaped leaves at their tip. The flower spikes with their medium to very large flowers appear from the base of the pseudobulbs and are slightly arched or sometimes pendulous. The wax-like and very long-lasting flowers consist of expanded sepals and petals, which look identical, and a tri-lobed lip, usually of a different colour and protruding. The natural distribution area stretches from the Himalaya region to Indochina, South China, Japan and Indonesia to Australia. Whereas true species are not often cultivated, there are over one thousand artificial hybrids from which the orchid grower can choose. *Cymbidium* hybrids can nowadays be bought as cut flowers in the most varied colour combinations from nearly every florist. The beautiful, large flower spikes last a relatively long time, even when cut.
Cultivation Most *Cymbidium* species are cultivated as semi-terrestrial plants, even if they grow as epiphytes in nature. The cymbidiums have a strong root growth and require a relatively large pot so that there is sufficient room for their roots, and good drainage to avoid the roots standing in permanent moisture. Wooden baskets are also suitable for species with pendulous spikes. Compost is a mixture of osmunda or tree-fern fibre, chopped sphagnum moss and coarse, white sand. During the growing period in summer they require a lot of water and high humidity. As soon as the new pseudobulbs have stopped growing, they are kept under drier and cooler conditions. This rest period stretches over several weeks and is needed to encourage flowering. During this period they should nevertheless occasionally be watered, so that neither pseudobulbs nor leaves shrivel or wither. As soon as the flower buds are clearly visible, regular and normal watering must be

resumed. The leaves do not really tolerate direct and strong sunshine, so that a shady, but if possible light place should be chosen. Most cymbidiums, including the species to be described, require intermediate conditions during the growing period and cool conditions for the remainder of the time. The plants are best kept throughout the summer until autumn on the balcony or in the garden (provided there is shade). A few cool nights (without frost!) during the autumn have even a favourable effect on the flowering. They must be kept in a cool room until flowering in spring. *Cymbidium* species from Indonesia and Australia require continually warm conditions. Repotting is done in spring when required after flowering. New plants can be cultivated from the back-bulbs.

Cymbidium devonianum
Characteristics   This species, named after the Duke of Devonshire, because he was the first grower in Europe to bring this plant to flower, normally has stunted pseudobulbs which are hidden behind the leaves. The three to five leaves per new pseudobulb are 20–35 cm (8–14 in) long, rather wide and with rounded-off apices. Near the pseudobulb they reduce to a stem. The strong, arching flower spike reaches about 30 cm (12 in), and its numerous (up to ten) flowers form close together. The thick flowers, approximately 3 cm ($1\frac{1}{4}$ in) in diameter, have elongated, egg-shaped, olive-green to light brown sepals and petals with violet spots or stripes, and a fleshy, broadly egg-shaped lip, which is light to dark violet with very dark violet patches on each side lobe. The column is bent forwards and is yellow.

Habitat   Himalaya region; at altitudes of approximately 1500 m (5000 ft).

Flowering season   Spring, summer.

Cymbidium tigrinum
Characteristics   The egg-shaped, closely arranged pseudobulbs reach a length of 2.5–3 cm ($1–1\frac{1}{4}$ in). The three to five, slightly bent, strap-shaped and pointed leaves are 8–15 cm (3–6 in) long and about 2 cm ($\frac{3}{4}$ in) wide. The flower spike is slim, either erect or slightly arching and grows to

Cymbidium devonianum (× 3)

Cymbidium tigrinum (5/6 nat. size)

20 cm (8 in); it carries three to six widely spaced flowers, 6–9 cm (2½–3½ in) diameter. The tongue-shaped, pointed sepals and petals are olive-green with red spots towards the base. The lip is tri-lobed and has roundish, upright side lobes, which are yellow with wide, red-brown stripes, and an oval tapering, white central lobe, which arches downwards and has short, purple-brown horizontal lines, giving it a tiger-like (= *tigrinum*) appearance. The column bends forwards and is olive-green with red spots.

Habitat   Burma; on rocks at altitudes of 1700–2000 m (5660–6660 ft).

Flowering season   Spring.

Bifrenaria

Tr. Maxillarieae Subtr. Lycastinae

Etymology   From (Lat.) *bi-* = two-, *frenum* = reins; the four pollinia sit separately on two stems.

Description   This genus comprises nearly 30 species which are all found in South America and in particular in Brazil. The egg-shaped pseudobulbs grow closely together and carry a single deciduous leaf each. The relatively large flowers are not very numerous and appear from the base of the pseudobulbs.

Cultivation   Being epiphytic, these species are best cultivated in a mixture of osmunda fibre and sphagnum moss in pots or meshed baskets. During their growing period they require an intermediate to warm and light situation. Sufficient watering and a fairly high humidity are of advantage during this period. After ripening of the new pseudobulb, a rest period of several weeks is required without much water and under intermediate and shady conditions so as to induce flowering. Repotting should be carried out infrequently as the plants do not tolerate disturbance.

Bifrenaria vitellina

syn. *Stenocoryne vitellina*

Characteristics   This species is closely related to *B. racemosa* and is very similar to it. The flower stem grows to 20 cm (8 in) and carries five to eight widely spaced flowers, approximately 1.5 cm (½ in) in diameter. They do not open very widely, but more widely than *B. racemosa*, and are yellow-orange to light-brown in colour. The tri-lobed

Bifrenaria vitellina (× 4)

yellow (= *vitellina*) lip is covered with hairs on the inside and has at the base of the undulated front lobe a large, dark purple patch. The side lobes enclose the white column.
Habitat Brazil.
Flowering season Autumn.

Lycaste

Tr. Maxillarieae Subtr. Lycastinae
Etymology Named after Lycaste, the beautiful daughter of the Greek king Priam.
Description The genus comprises approximately 35 species which are usually epiphytic orchids with nearly egg-shaped, sometimes flattened pseudobulbs. The large, comparatively thin and folded leaves are shed yearly. The often large and very handsome flowers usually appear singly on stems of varying length which grow from the base of older pseudobulbs. In relation to the large sepals, which dominate the flower, the lip is rather small. The petals normally stand outwards parallel with the column, and are differently coloured from the sepals. *Lycaste* species are found mainly in the mountain regions of the American tropics from Mexico to Brazil.

Cultivation Although *Lycaste* species grow in the wild both at sea-level and in higher mountain regions so that the temperature range is wide, they prefer intermediate conditions when cultivated. During the rest period, when watering is reduced to just enough to ensure that the pseudobulbs do not shrivel, they can be stood in a somewhat cooler place. All lycastes like light, but require shade and sufficient air circulation. During the growing period until they shed their leaves, watering should be regular and adequate but must be allowed to drain off. A good drainage from broken crocks is therefore important. Compost for pot culture is usually a mixture of leaf mould and garden soil (with chopped beech leaves), osmunda fibre and sphagnum moss, as is used for terrestrial orchids. The best time to repot is after flowering.

Lycaste aromatica
Characteristics The 6–8 cm (2½–3 in) high, egg-shaped and flattish pseudobulbs are enclosed by sheaths at their base. The pseudobulbs bear one or two leaves, 25–40 cm (10–16 in) long and 10 cm (4

Lycaste aromatica (nat. size)

Lycaste fimbriata (× 1.5)

in) wide; they are lanceolate, folded and pointed. Flower stems are erect and 10–15 cm (4–6 in) long, bearing a single flower, though several stems usually appear on a plant. They carry a wax-like, aromatic (= *aromatica*) flower with a lemony scent and have a diameter of 6–8 cm (2½–3 in). The elliptical, about 3 cm (1¼ in) long sepals are greenish yellow and extend radially. The slightly shorter, elliptical petals are a brilliant orange-yellow, stand horizontally and are recurved. The tri-lobed lip has an erect, longish side lobe and a usually elliptical to roundish central lobe which is turned downwards and slightly undulated around its edge, sometimes extending to a tongue-shaped tip. The lip is orange-yellow with some red spots and carries in its centre a grooved callus.
Habitat Mexico to Honduras.
Flowering season Usually spring.

Lycaste fimbriata
syn. *Lycaste costata*
Characteristics The close-standing, egg-shaped and 10–15 cm (4–6 in) long pseudobulbs form grooves with aging, and usually carry two large leaves (approximately 40 cm (16 in) long and 8 cm (3 in) wide), which are lanceolate, folded and rather rigid. Several flower stems are usually formed, growing to 10–15 cm (4–6 in) and carrying one wax-like, beautifully scented flower, each about 10 cm (4 in) across, which last for several weeks. The colour of the flower is uniformly ivory-white to greenish white, only the callus on the lip being tinted slightly yellow. Of the elongated pointed sepals, the central sepal curves slightly forward, whereas the lateral sepals spread downward in a sickle-shape. The tri-lobed lip has elongated, blunted side lobes and a broadly elliptical central lobe which is finely fringed (= *fimbriata*) around the edge, and the tip of which hangs slightly down.
Habitat Peru.
Flowering season Spring.

Maxillaria
Tr. Maxillarieae Subtr. Maxillariinae
Etymology *Maxilla* (Lat.) = jaw; referring to the shape of the lip base.

Description Most of the around 200 *Maxillaria* species are epiphytes with the exception of a few lithophytes. The distribution area reaches from south Florida, Mexico and the Antilles to Argentina and Brazil. In view of this wide distribution, the differences in habit are obviously considerable. They can be roughly divided into two groups. One group possesses clearly visible pseudobulbs which arise from the creeping rhizome in close formation. With some of this group the rhizome grows upright so that the pseudobulbs are arranged in tiers. With the other group the pseudobulbs are hardly visible or are non-existent. These species have either erect stems with leaves in pairs or, in a few cases, stemless clusters of leaves in the shape of a fan similar to irises. With maxillarias the flower stem, never carrying more than one flower, rises from the base of the pseudobulbs or from the leaf axils. Characteristic of this genus is the manner in which the base of the column and the fused base of the lateral sepals form a 'jaw' (hence the name). The sepals and the smaller petals are elongated. The lip is usually tri-lobed and turned slightly downwards.
Cultivation Most of the cultivated *Maxillaria* species and those described below come from higher mountain regions and therefore require intermediate conditions. During the growing period in summer watering should be plentiful. They love a rather high humidity, plenty of fresh air and a shady place so that the leaves do not scorch. A short rest period is advisable to induce flowering. Apart from this, maxillarias do not require an extended rest during winter. Slightly less watering is beneficial, but the compost should not be left to dry out too much. The smaller the pseudobulbs, the more damaging is an excessive drying out. Compost for pot culture is a mixture of osmunda fibre and sphagnum moss. Adequate drainage must be ensured. Some types can also be cultivated on tree-fern slabs or on bark with a little compost. Most *Maxillaria* species are relatively easily cared for.

Maxillaria picta
Characteristics This charming species is the one most frequently cultivated. It possesses egg-shaped, compressed, approximately 6 cm (2½ in) high pseudobulbs which form fairly close together

Maxillaria picta (× 2)

on the rhizome and develop grooves with aging. The single leaves (rarely two together) are tongue-shaped and 25–30 cm (10–12 in) long. The slim, erect flower stem 12–20 cm (4¾–8 in) long, carries a robust, about 6 cm (2½ in) single flower which lasts very well. Several flower stems issue simultaneously from each pseudobulb. The strap-shaped, pointed sepals curl forwards into a quarter circle. Their colour is brilliant golden yellow within and on the outside yellowish white with some brown-violet spots (*picta* = colourful spotting). The shorter and narrower petals stand nearly parallel to the column and have the same colour as the sepals. The lip is tri-lobed and yellowish white with red spots at the base. The side lobes tend upwards, and the tongue-shaped central lobe slightly downwards. The column is a beautiful red-violet. *M. punctata* Lodd. has the same habitat and a very similar appearance to the type described above, but is a little smaller.

Habitat Brazil.

Flowering season Winter, spring.

Maxillaria sophronitis

syn. *Ornithidium sophronitis*

Characteristics This is a dwarf, creeping species. Its two-leaved, oval and approximately 2 cm ($\frac{3}{4}$ in) pseudobulbs form on the branched rhizome at intervals of 1–2 cm ($\frac{1}{8}$–$\frac{3}{4}$ in). The rather fleshy, elongated and blunted leaves grow to roughly 2.5 cm (1 in). The single flowers appear from the base of the pseudobulbs on an approximately 3 cm ($1\frac{1}{4}$ in) stem. The attractive flowers are a brilliant scarlet, about 2 cm ($\frac{3}{4}$ in) across and similar to the genus *Sophronitis* (*sophron* = modest). The oval and pointed, about 1 cm ($\frac{3}{8}$ in) long sepals and the slightly shorter petals curve forwards in a bell-shape. The golden yellow lip turns sharply downwards and is about as long as the petals.

Habitat Colombia, Venezuela; at altitudes of 800–1600 m (2660–5330 ft).

Flowering season Spring and autumn.

Maxillaria tenuifolia

Characteristics A climbing rhizome carries egg-shaped, somewhat compressed pseudobulbs, around 2.5 cm (1 in) long and 2–3 cm ($\frac{3}{4}$–$1\frac{1}{4}$ in) apart. The delicate, narrow dark green leaves (*tenuifolia* = delicate leaves) grow 25–35 cm (10–14 in) long and approximately 1 cm ($\frac{3}{8}$ in) wide, and have a central groove on the upper side. Each pseudobulb usually develops several thin flower stems of approximately 5 cm (2 in) which carry well-scented and robust single flowers, 4–5 cm ($1\frac{1}{2}$–2 in) across. The egg-shaped to lanceolate, spreading sepals, are revolute around the margin, and

Maxillaria sophronitis (× 2)

Maxillaria tenuifolia (× 2.5)

the somewhat shorter, tongue-shaped petals, projecting forward in parallel with the column, are dark red with yellow spotting towards the base. The elongated, blunted lip is angled downwards towards the tip and flecked yellow and dark red to red-brown. The wedge-shaped column is pale yellow with dark red spots at the front.

Habitat Mexico to Honduras and Nicaragua.

Flowering season Usually summer.

Comparettia

Tr. Oncidieae Subtr. Comparettiinae

Etymology Named after the Italian botanist Andreo Comparetti (18th century).

Description This genus contains around twelve species which are all to be found in tropical Central America at intermediate altitudes. All species have rather large, attractive, brilliantly coloured flowers on multifloral racemes. They have thin pseudobulbs, from the base of which the inflorescence appears. The flower structure is uniform for all species. The upper sepal and the petals spread out;

the lateral sepals are fused together up to their tip and extend backwards from the base into a long, slim spur. The large lip is slit at the front, forming two kidney-shaped side lobes. At the base of the lip there are two small appendages which continue into the sepal spur. The column is spherical on top and carries the pollinia on a short stem.

Cultivation In view of their habitat, *Comparettia* species thrive in steady intermediate conditions. As the cylindrical pseudobulbs are rather small, the fleshy leaves sometimes take over the task of storing nutrients. The plants therefore cannot withstand prolonged dryness and a fairly constant moistness of the compost and humidity of around 70% should be maintained. After flowering there is a very short rest period with reduced watering. However, as soon as the new growths appear, plentiful watering must be resumed without however creating stagnant conditions. Direct sunlight is not easily tolerated by these plants with their thick, but relatively soft foliage. They nevertheless require a light situation close to the glass. They can be cultivated on cork with a little compost or on tree-fern slabs with a little sphagnum moss, and in

Comparettia macroplectrum (natural size)

small pots with very good drainage through broken crocks. Compost for pot culture is a mixture of tree-fern or osmunda fibre with chopped sphagnum moss. To prevent the fine roots from completely drying out, the pots can be covered with living sphagnum moss. On warm days the exposed roots welcome syringing. The flower stems should not be cut off immediately after flowering because side branches can occur from the dormant bracts which will bloom again.

Comparettia macroplectrum
Characteristics The thin, elongated and compressed pseudobulbs are about 2 cm ($\frac{3}{4}$ in) long and carry a single dark green leaf. The erect, elongated and pointed leaves are usually up to 12 cm ($4\frac{3}{4}$ in) long. The loosely arranged inflorescence, growing out of the sheaths enclosing the pseudobulbs, is arched, sometimes branched, and reaches a length of more than 50 cm (20 in). The flowers are around 5 cm (2 in) across and bloom consecutively. They are 8–25 in number, depending on the length of the inflorescence and the number of branches. The single blooms keep for two to three weeks. All parts

of the flower are whitish to light violet with dark violet spots which are slightly less pronounced on the lip. The lip is incised at its tip. The slim, nearly erect and rather large sepal spur (= *macroplectrum*) reaches 5 cm (2 in) and is whitish to brownish or greenish.
Habitat Colombia.
Flowering season Autumn.

Comparettia speciosa
Characteristics This lesser-known *Comparettia* species reaches an overall maximum height of around 20 cm (8 in), of which at least 16–18 cm ($6\frac{3}{8}$–7 in) are accounted for by the erect, leathery and slightly crinkled leaves. The branching inflorescence of up to 50 cm (20 in) develops from the base of the pseudobulbs and arches over with its loosely arranged flowers on few branches. It carries, depending on its length, six to 25 magnificent (= *speciosa*) flowers about 3 cm ($1\frac{1}{4}$ in) in diameter. The elliptical petals, with pointed ends and the upper sepal of similar shape, are about 1.5 cm ($\frac{1}{2}$ in) long and have a yellowish basic colour with red veins. The nearly 3 cm ($1\frac{1}{4}$ in) wide front

Comparettia speciosa (× 1.6)

Gongora armeniaca (× 1.4)

lobe of the lip, raised as with *C. falcata*, has the same shape and colour as *C. coccinea*. The slim, greenish yellow sepal spur grows to around 4 cm (1½ in) and curves just slightly.

Habitat Ecuador.

Flowering season Spring.

Gongora

Tr. Oncidieae Subtr. Gongorinae

Etymology Named after the Spanish Bishop Don Antonio Caballero y Gongora.

Description There are about twenty epiphytic species in this genus, which are recognized by their bizarre shape, reminding us of the artistry of wrought-iron work. Their distribution area is tropical Central and South America. The egg-shaped, grooved pseudobulbs normally carry two leaves. The flower spikes, in some species bearing an abundance of flowers and in others just a few, appear from the base of the pseudobulbs and are pendulous, for which reason the lip of the blooms points upwards. The ovary with the flower stem together form an up-turned semi-circle. The flowers usually have a pleasant scent and strong colouring. The lateral sepals are reflexed or rolled up and stand out horizontally. The central sepal is partly joined to the back of the column. The petals are much smaller than the sepals and also

fuse with the rear of the column. As the flowers always hang upside down due to their pendulous growth, the slightly bent column lies below the lip.

Cultivation Because of their trusses of flowers, *Gongora* species must be cultivated in hanging pots or wooden baskets. The usual mixture of osmunda or tree-fern fibre with sphagnum moss is a good well-drained compost, to which can be added small pieces of tree bark. The plants require humidity at all times and have no strict rest period. For ripening of the pseudobulbs and encouragement of flowers, watering is somewhat reduced for a short time. *Gongora* species are best kept in semi-shady and intermediate conditions. In summer they can be placed on the balcony or in the garden. Buds and flowers are very sensitive to direct contact with water, so that the inflorescence must at no time be syringed, otherwise the flowers may stain or drop prematurely.

Gongora armeniaca

Characteristics The pseudobulbs of this species grow 5–6 cm (2–2½ in) long. Two elongated, pointed leaves grow from the pseudobulb on a thinnish stem and reach approximately 25 cm (10 in) in length and 5 cm (2 in) in width. The inflorescence carries loosely arranged flowers, ten to 15 in number, and grows to an overall length of 30 cm (12 in). The wax-like, approximately 5 cm (2 in) flowers have a scent reminiscent of apricots, and are a drab yellow or orange colour, sometimes with violet-brown mottling. The two lateral sepals stand sideways; the concave central sepal points downwards and has an elliptical and pointed shape. The short, lanceolate petals are joined only at the base of the column; they taper towards their ends and are sometimes curved inwards. The fleshy and roundish lip ends in a point with a beak-like appendage. The top of the column usually extends into a club-shape.

Habitat Nicaragua.

Flowering season Summer to autumn.

Ionopsis

Tr. Oncidieae Subtr. Ionopsidinae

Etymology From (Gr.) *ion* = violet; *opsis* = similar; referring to the similarity of the flowers to those of violets.

Description This species is reminiscent in appearance of the *Comparettia* genus and consists of 4 species which all have their origins in tropical America from Florida to Brazil. However, only the species described below has so far been cultivated.

Cultivation *Ionopsis* species, originating from lowish mountain regions, require intermediate to warm conditions. Regular watering is necessary as they do not have any pseudobulbs as such. It is advisable to place them in a very light position so as to obtain colourful flowers, but direct sunshine should be avoided. They are best cultivated in small pots filled with well drained osmunda fibre, tree-fern fibre or pieces of bark. They can also be planted on pieces of tree-fern. Repotting should be carried out infrequently because of the very delicate root system. The old flower spikes should not be cut off after flowering, as they can branch out and flower again.

Ionopsis utricularioides

syn. *Ionopsis paniculata*

Characteristics This charming species can vary greatly as regards size of the plant, its flowers and their colour. The stunted, cylindrical pseudobulbs are 1–1.5 cm ($\frac{3}{8}$–$\frac{1}{2}$ in) high with no leaves growing from their apex. They are enclosed usually by three lanceolate and fleshy leaves, 10–15 cm (4–6 in) long, and about 2 cm ($\frac{3}{4}$ in) wide. The flower

Ionopsis utricularioides (3/4 nat. size)

panicle (= *paniculata*) grows from the leaf axils, is pendulous and reaches 50–80 cm (20–32 in), carrying a multitude of flowers. As the 1.5–2 cm ($\frac{3}{8}$–$\frac{3}{4}$ in) blooms flower consecutively, the overall flowering period is approximately two weeks. The colour ranges from the pure white to a strong purple with all shades in between. The flowers are most commonly whitish to light violet with violet veining on the lip. Sepals and petals are very small in contrast to the large, inverted heart-shaped lip. The central sepal and the petals form a small hood.

Habitat South Florida, Mexico to Brazil and Paraguay, West Indies.

Flowering season Usually autumn to winter.

Rodriguezia

Tr. Oncidieae Subtr. Ionopsidinae

Etymology Named after the Spanish botanist Rodriguez (18th/19th century).

Description Around thirty attractive species, most of them epiphytes, are contained in this genus. They are distributed from Nicaragua to Peru and Brazil. In Brazil alone there are about twenty species. The small, narrow, one- to two-leaved pseudobulbs grow from the rhizome either closely together or spaced apart, and are usually hidden behind their comparatively large and leaf-like sheaths, between which emerges the inflorescence. An attractive feature is that strong plants can form more than one spike, some with few and others with many flowers. The central sepal and the petals are very similar and bow downwards together. The two lateral sepals are joined together, sometimes strongly, with a cup-shaped hollow at the base and are hidden behind the bi-lobed lip which projects downwards and broadens out. The short column sometimes carries horn-like appendages.

Cultivation *Rodriguezia* species can be grown in pots or in wooden baskets and also on tree-fern slabs and cork bark, but being epiphytic orchids, they prefer the latter because of their aerial roots. Compost is a mixture of osmunda or tree-fern fibre with a little chopped sphagnum moss. As the roots do not tolerate stagnation, the compost must be open and the container must have good drainage. Rodriguezias usually grow throughout the year without a rest period and therefore require continually copious watering. They should be placed in an intermediate to warm spot, which must be light but not too sunny and airy. A relatively high humidity is advantageous. If the temperature is reduced during flowering, the flowers will last for several weeks. The numerous, fine aerial roots can be sprayed daily to encourage growth, but they must be dry by the evening.

Rodriguezia decora
Characteristics The wire-like rhizome, up to 0.5 m (20 in) long and clinging to its base by numerous thin roots, carries at intervals of up to 10 cm (4 in) almost circular, flat and single-leaved pseudobulbs, approximately 3 cm ($1\frac{1}{4}$ in) long. The leaves, up to 10 cm (4 in) long and 2.5 cm (1 in) wide, have an elongated and pointed shape and are rather leathery. The loosely arranged, slightly pendulons inflorescence reaches 30–40 cm (12–16 in) and is decorated (= *decora*) with twenty or more slightly scented and beautiful 4 cm ($1\frac{1}{2}$ in) flowers. The elongated, pointed sepals and petals form a tube projecting forwards with a white to yellowish base mottled red-violet inside and out. The two lateral sepals are joined and form a rear spur, approximately 2 mm ($\frac{1}{16}$ in) long. The relatively large lip stands out from the tube. The lip is narrow at the base and broadens outwards into a kidney-shape with a deep division. This kidney-shaped part is white, the base being white with red-violet spotted keels.

Rodriguezia decora (× 3)

Habitat Brazil.
Flowering season Autumn.

Rodriguezia secunda (nat. size)

Rodriguezia secunda

Characteristics The elongated, elliptical, flat and closely arranged pseudobulbs grow 3–5 cm ($1\frac{1}{4}$–2 in) high. They are nearly completely hidden by leaf-like sheaths. The two to three leathery, strap-shaped leaves, usually folded lengthwise, reach 15–20 cm (6–8 in), being approximately 2 cm ($\frac{3}{4}$ in) wide. Several pendulous inflorescences, each with many, closely arranged flowers, issue from each new growth and grow as long as the leaf. The rose-red flowers, about 1.5 cm ($\frac{1}{2}$ in) in size, all turn in the same direction ($= secunda$). The oval and pointed sepals and petals form a hood over the entire lip which is pendulous; the lip itself is oval with a rim along its slightly undulating margin and has a keel at its base. The two lateral sepals are joined together and hidden behind the lip.

Habitat Panama, Venezuela, Colombia to Brazil and also Trinidad.

Flowering season Usually late spring/summer, sometimes also several times during the year.

Lockhartia

Tr. Oncidieae Subtr. Lockhartiinae

Etymology Named after the English botanist David Lockhart (19th century).

Description This genus covers around thirty epiphytic species from tropical America. A characteristic of these species is the lack of pseudobulbs and the erect stems which are closely covered with fleshy leaves which have a plaited appearance due to their distichous arrangement. The attractive flowers usually appear singly or in racemes in the leaf axils towards the tops of the stems and are very similar to the *Oncidium* genus. Each stem elongates apically for several years continuing to give blooms. Sepals and petals spread out and sometimes turn inwards. The lip is usually tri-lobed with two small side lobes and a large divided front lobe featuring in its centre wart-like growths.

Cultivation *Lockhartia* species grow well in pots or wooden baskets with plenty of broken crocks and a compost of osmunda or tree-fern fibre and a little sphagnum moss. As the roots do not tolerate too much compost, they can also be cultivated on a piece of bark with osmunda fibre and sphagnum moss or on a piece of tree-fern. They should be placed in an intermediate to warm spot in semi-shade, and sufficient, but not excessive humidity must be ensured. The plants should not be divided too often, as only strong plants flower well. A rest period is not required so that regular watering is necessary, without however creating stagnation.

Lockhartia oerstedii

Characteristics This species, named after Oersted, has 30 cm (12 in) and longer flat stems, densely covered with triangular leaves, 2–3 cm ($\frac{3}{4}$–$1\frac{1}{4}$ in) long. The very short inflorescence carrying one to four flowers, emerges from the leaf axils at the top of the stem. Along the peduncles, nearly as far as the approximately 2 cm ($\frac{3}{4}$ in) large, brilliantly yellow flowers, and also at the branching out points of the racemes, are relatively large, heart-shaped bracts (around 8 mm ($\frac{5}{16}$ in) long). The sepals are oval with the lateral sepals turned sharply backwards. The narrow oval petals, spreading sideways, are bent to form a chute angled backwards. The complicated lip structure hangs downwards and has red-brown markings at the base against a yellow background. The elon-

Lockhartia oerstedii (× 1.4)

gated, very thin base lobes of the lip project sideways and bend forwards in a semi-circle. The front lobe diverges at its tip, has an inverted heart-shape with very pronounced wart-like central calli which are a yellow-orange. At the side of these warts are the two small triangular side lobes bent backwards. As regards habit and appearance of flowers, this species is very similar to *L. lunifera*, which can however be identified by the stems which grow to a maximum length of 20 cm (8 in) and the heart-shaped sheaths which grow to only 3–4 mm ($\frac{1}{8}$–$\frac{5}{32}$ in). The lip is the same basic shape, but the base lobes and the front lobe are a little broader; also the less pronounced warts in the lip centre are rather camouflaged by the red-brown lip marking. *L. lunifera* is found only in Brazil.

Habitat Central America.

Flowering season Throughout the year, usually summer.

Brassia

Tr. Oncidieae Subtr. Oncidiinae

Etymology Named after the researcher and plant collector William Brass (19th century).

Description This genus comprises nearly forty epiphytic species, which are not readily distinguishable from each other and are all found in tropical America, from south Florida via Mexico to Brazil. *Brassia* species have oval and rather flattish pseudobulbs, bearing one or two narrow, thick leaves at the top. The flower buds appear from the base of the young pseudobulbs; they are protected by a sheath and usually reach a considerable length. In view of their spidery shape, this species is also commonly called the 'spider orchid', the long and very thin petals and sepals resembling spiders' legs. The flowers smell pleasantly, particularly during the middle of the day, and form a loose scape.

Cultivation During the growing period (spring to autumn) *Brassia* species require plenty of water.

Brassia verrucosa (3/4 nat. size)

They also require good light (but no scorching sunshine), a humid atmosphere and good air circulation. The room must be kept intermediate (to warm) during this time. As the growing season ends, watering should be slowly reduced to allow the pseudobulbs to ripen. During the rest period brassias are kept a little cooler and drier. Premature growth during winter must be avoided if flowers are to be obtained the following year. Being epiphytic plants, they are best planted in baskets, as this allows the roots to be exposed. Compost is a mixture of osmunda or chopped tree-fern fibre and sphagnum moss. Repotting becomes necessary when the compost is old and stale, because the roots cannot tolerate this.

Brassia verrucosa
Characteristics The pseudobulbs are very heavily compressed, oval with faint lengthwise grooves, being about 10 cm (4 in) long and 5 cm (2 in) wide. Leaves form around the base, but these are somewhat smaller than the two which issue from the tip of the bulb. They are leathery, lanceolate and pointed, with a central fold, approximately 30 cm (12 in) long and 5 cm (2 in) wide. The flower stem is straight and grows to around 60 cm (24 in). The five to fifteen longlasting flowers grow 20 – 25 cm (8 – 10 in) long. The radiating, slightly twisted, thin and tapering sepals are light green with some dark green to brownish spots of varying size at the base. The petals are similar, but a little shorter. The lip is violin-shaped, leading to a point, and only 3–4 cm ($1\frac{1}{4}$–$1\frac{1}{2}$ in) long; it has dark green, wart-like (= *verrucosa*) spots towards its centre and a slightly undulated rim.
Habitat Mexico to Venezuela.
Flowering season Spring, summer.

Miltonia

Tr. Oncidieae Subtr. Oncidiinae
Etymology Named after the English orchid enthusiast Lord Fitzwilliam Milton (1786—1857).
Description The *Miltonia* genus contains around twenty species and a few natural hybrids. All miltonias are epiphytes from Central and South America ranging from Costa Rica to Ecuador and Brazil. Most species have short, well-formed pseudobulbs, which carry one to three rather narrow leaves. The single- or multi-flowered inflorescence stands erect and appears from the base of the latest pseudobulb. The flat flowers, lasting on a plant for four to six weeks, are large and are very similar to pansies. The large, undivided lip has at its base some short keels. There are numerous artificial *Miltonia* hybrids, and intergeneric hybrids with other genera such as *Odontoglossum* and *Oncidium*.

Cultivation *Miltonia* species have two main distribution regions, the first being in Brazil where they grow together with cattleyas, and the second being in the Colombian Andes, now more correctly known as *Miltonopsis*. The Brazilian species are cultivated under intermediate conditions. Species from Columbia must be kept cool in the same way as odontoglossums. Most miltonias can be well cared for in pots or wooden baskets containing a compost for epiphytic orchids, i.e. mainly a mixture of osmunda fibre and sphagnum moss. Good drainage is essential. The compost should not be compressed too firmly, so that sufficient air can reach the roots. Species with climbing rhizomes grow best on tree-fern slabs or on cork bark with a little compost. During the growing season, which commences with new root action, watering should be plentiful. In the winter rest period watering should be restricted although the compost must not be left to dry out completely for any length of time. The plants also require a relatively high humidity with sufficient air circulation, in particular the varieties from the misty forests of Colombia which grow at high altitudes. Miltonias require less light than cattleyas so that the best place is in semi-shade.

Miltonia clowesii
Characteristics This species was named after the Englishman John Clowes and he was the first to achieve flowering in Europe. The oval, compressed, 7–10 cm ($2\frac{3}{4}$–4 in) high pseudobulbs grow at short intervals along the rhizome and carry 2 strap-shaped, pointed leaves 30–45 cm (12–18 in) long. The 50 cm (20 in) flower stem is straight, but sometimes arches under the weight of the seven to ten closely arranged flowers, each about 7 cm ($2\frac{3}{4}$ in) across. Sepals and petals look alike, being tongue-shaped, pointed, slightly undulated and

Miltonia clowesii (× 2)

around 3.5 cm ($1\frac{3}{8}$ in) long, yellow to light brown in colour with large dark brown stripes and patches. The lip is 3–4 cm ($1\frac{1}{4}$–$1\frac{1}{2}$ in) long, constricted in the centre, giving a violin shape, and has a violet colouring towards the base with two longer and two shorter keels. The front part of the lip is creamy white and turns to yellow after the bloom has been in flower for some time.

Habitat Brazil.

Flowering season Autumn.

Odontoglossum

Tr. Oncidieae Subtr. Oncidiinae

Etymology From *odontos* (Gr.) = tooth, *glossa* = tongue; referring to the tooth-like parts on the lip.

Description The genus *Odontoglossum* contains approximately 100 species which are almost exclusively epiphytic. Their habitat is the higher mountains (about 1500–3000 m (5000–10000 ft)) of tropical Central and northern South America. Some species grow at such high altitudes that they are sometimes exposed to temperatures near freezing point for short periods. All *Odontoglossum* species have closely arranged, egg-shaped and laterally compressed pseudobulbs, usually surrounded by sheaths at their bases, and bearing at their apex one to three leaves. The paniculate inflorescence springs from the foot of the pseudobulb and is usually erect or arched, but seldom pendulous. A special characteristic of odontoglossums, unlike their close relatives, the oncidiums, is the manner in which the lip base grows almost parallel to the column and has tooth-like nodules, with the front lobe and lip base at right angles to each other. The slim column protrudes and carries on each side a wing-shaped or ear-shaped appendage. With their beautiful and attractive flowers, many *Odontoglossum* species have been used in the crossing of several thousand hybrids.

Cultivation Most *Odontoglossum* species grow best under cool conditions, although one notable exception is *O. krameri*, which requires intermediate conditions. Success depends very much on maintaining low temperatures, in particular during the rest period in winter. Coming from misty tropical forests, they require a relatively moist atmosphere and plenty of ventilation. During the rest period watering should be restricted. In the growing season in summer they must be kept as cool as possible, by shading, evaporative cooling, syringing the plants and their surroundings, and an increase in ventilation on cooler nights. Regular and plentiful watering is essential during this time. In autumn, the ripening time for the pseudobulbs and for encouraging flowering, the plants can be kept completely dry until the inflorescence appears. When in flower, a little more water should be given. Being epiphytes, all odontoglossums require a compost of osmunda fibre and sphagnum moss in which they are planted in a pot with good drainage. As with most orchids, they are very vulnerable to sogginess around the roots. A suitable time for repotting is when roots start to grow in spring.

Odontoglossum bictoniense

Characteristics This species was brought to flower for the first time in Europe by Lord Rolle in Bicton (= *bictoniense*). It has oval, flattish pseudobulbs, 12–15 cm ($4\frac{3}{4}$–6 in) long, which are surrounded by sheaths and carry two to three leaves. The leaves grow up to 45 cm (18 in) and are elongated elliptical, pointed and soft. The stiffly erect flower stem grows 60 to 100 cm (24–40 in) topped by eight to twelve flowers, each 4–5 cm ($1\frac{1}{2}$–2 in) in diameter. The lanceolate sepals are about 2 cm ($\frac{3}{4}$ in) long and bend slightly at the tip, their colour being yellowish green with red-brown patches. The petals are the same colour and shape, but a little shorter than the sepals. The heart-shaped to triangular lip is a little longer than the sepals, undulated around the margin and shaded white to light violet. At its base it has a short, narrow nodule on which are two yellowish keels.

Habitat Mexico, Guatemala.

Flowering season Autumn to spring.

Odontoglossum cervantesii

Characteristics This is a dwarf variety dedicated to the Mexican professor of botany, Cinventio Cervantes. The egg-shaped, single-leaved pseudobulbs grow densely together and are 3–5 cm ($1\frac{1}{4}$–2 in) high. The elongated elliptical to lanceolate leaves are rather narrow and reach lengths of 10–15 cm (4–6 in). The erect or slightly arching inflorescence, not more than 25–30 cm (10–12 in) high, carries one to six scented flowers, about 6 cm ($2\frac{1}{2}$ in) across, and is covered with small, brownish bracts. The broadly lanceolate sepals and petals, radiating in star formation, are about 3 cm ($1\frac{1}{4}$ in) long and have a white or occasionally violet-pink basic colour and towards their base concentric red-brown to violet stripes. The basic colouring of the lip is similar to other parts of the flower and the lip has at its base a short, narrow nodule with small,

Odontoglossum bictoniense (4/5 nat. size)

Odontoglossum cervantesii (1/2 nat. size)

yellow protuberances continuing into a large egg- to heart-shaped front lobe, which is undulated around its edge. The white to yellowish column carries at the front on both sides an ear-shaped appendage.

Habitat Central America.

Flowering season Late autumn, winter.

Odontoglossum cordatum

Characteristics The single-leaved, 6–8 cm ($2\frac{1}{2}$–3 in) pseudobulbs are of a flat, elongated egg-shape and stand close together. The elongated elliptical to lanceolate, leathery leaves are folded at their base and 20–30 cm (8–12 in) long and around 4.5 cm ($1\frac{3}{4}$ in) wide. The flower stem is normally erect and reaches approximately 40 cm (16 in), carrying at its head five to eight flowers, 6–8 cm ($2\frac{1}{2}$–3 in) in diameter. The 5 cm (2 in) long sepals radiate and taper. They are yellowish to greenish with brown markings. The heart-shaped (= *cordatum*) lip has

Odontoglossum cordatum (nat. size)

Odontoglossum grande (3/4 nat. size)

at its base only a very short nodule with two yellowish to reddish keels. The lip is white with dense brown specks around the edge. The column has no ear-shaped appendages.

Habitat Mexico to Costa Rica.

Flowering season Usually summer, autumn.

Odontoglossum grande Tiger orchid

Characteristics The common name of this species with its large flowers refers to the stripes on the flowers. The pseudobulbs are roundish to egg-shaped and form grooves when aging. They grow to a height of 8–10 cm (3–4 in) and approximately 6 cm ($2\frac{1}{2}$ in) wide. The one to three lanceolate, short-stemmed leaves on each pseudobulb reach about 35 cm (14 in) long and 7 cm ($2\frac{3}{4}$ in) wide. The flower stem grows up to 30 cm (12 in) and carries three to eight loosely arranged, long-lasting and wax-like flowers, around 15 cm (6 in) in diameter. The tongue-shaped sepals are horizontally striped with red-brown against a basic yellow background. The petals are twice as wide as the sepals, have an undulating edge and are red-brown in colour from the base to the centre and yellow from the centre to the tip. The round to egg-shaped lip has an undulated margin and is only half as long as the sepals, having a whitish to yellowish background with light-brown transverse stripes around the base. At the base of the lip is a distinct, four-sided nodule, coloured yellow and reddish. The column has at the front two small semi-circular, pendant lobes.

Habitat Central America; at altitudes of up to 2500 m (8320 ft).

Flowering season Late autumn, winter.

Odontoglossum pulchellum
syn. *Osmoglossum pulchellum*.

Characteristics The narrow, elongated oval and

Odontoglossum pulchellum (1/2 nat. size)

densely formed pseudobulbs, 8–10 cm (3–4 in) long, bear at their apices two very narrow, strap-shaped leaves, approximately 30 cm (12 in) long and 1.5 cm ($\frac{1}{2}$ in) wide. The thin, flat flower stem grows 25–30 cm (10–12 in) long, stands erect or is slightly pendulous, and bears three to ten dainty (= *pulchellum*), pleasantly scented flowers, lasting around four weeks and approximately 3.5 cm ($1\frac{3}{8}$ in) in diameter. The flowers are not resupinated so that the lip points upwards. The elliptical, pointed sepals and petals are a pure white. The violin-shaped lip has at its base a brilliant yellow and red-brown dotted callus with two nodules, and a white front lobe projecting upwards and curving back at the apex. The 5 mm ($\frac{3}{16}$ in) long and white column is below and clearly tri-lobed.

Habitat Mexico, Guatemala, El Salvador; at altitudes of up to 2500 m (8320 ft).

Flowering season Autumn, winter.

Oncidium
Tr. Oncidieae Subtr. Oncidiinae

Etymology From *ogkos* (Gr.) (pronounced: onkos) = callosity; referring to the wart-like pro-tuberances on the lip base.

Description The genus *Oncidium*, comprising approximately 750 species, is a very varied one. The distribution area reaches from south Florida via Central America to Brazil and Argentina, with some species growing in warm, humid areas at sea-level, others at intermediate mountain levels and yet others in company with odontoglossums in higher and cooler mountain regions. With very few exceptions they are epiphytes. Oncidiums are very much favoured by orchid amateurs because their rich variety (more than fifty species being available commercially) offers types for all temperatures, many of them being relatively easily cared for and most of them having attractive flowers or flower panicles. They can be roughly divided into four groups according to their flowering habits. One group (e.g. *O. ornithorhynchum*) possesses clearly formed pseudobulbs with one or two leaves at their apices. A second group (e.g. *O. luridum*) has large, fleshy leaves which stand singly and only very small, stunted, inconspicuous pseudobulbs. The third group (e.g. *O. variegatum*) has very beautiful leaves arranged in a fan-shape without pseudobulbs. Finally, the last group (e.g. *O. cebolleta*) possesses grooved leaves of nearly circular cross-section, arising singly from the rhizome, and barely visible pseudobulbs. The flower spikes are usually branched and sometimes very long, carrying numerous flowers, generally of a yellow and brown colouring, although there are also white and reddish hues. All oncidiums have the same flower structure. Contrasted with related genera, they have a lip with several warts at the base which always forms a right angle with the short column. Both pollinia are spherical to egg-shaped.

Cultivation In view of their varying habitats, temperature requirements differ very greatly. Most of the commonly cultivated species however are best kept under intermediate conditions and of the species described on the following pages, only *O. krameranum* and *O. papilio* require warm conditions and *O. cucullatum* and *O. nubigenum* require cool conditions. Most oncidiums thrive in pots with good drainage, where they must be firmly planted in a compost of osmunda or tree-fern fibre with sphagnum and perhaps some dried beech-leaves. Pendulous species, or species with a creeping rhizome, are best planted on tree-fern slabs or on cork bark with a little compost. During the growing period watering should be plentiful, but for ripening of the pseudobulbs and for flower inducement and also during the winter rest period watering is hardly necessary. Species with under-developed pseudobulbs or those without pseudo-bulbs require particular care that the leaves do not shrink. Most species like sufficient humidity, plenty of ventilation and slight shade. Direct sunshine must be avoided so that the leaves do not scorch. The best repotting time is in early spring when the roots and new growths begin to emerge. Oncidiums can easily be propagated from back-bulbs.

Oncidium gardneri
Characteristics Named after Gardner, this type has egg-shaped, flat and bi-leaved pseudobulbs, 5–7 cm (2–2¾ in) long. The lanceolate, blunted leaves, growing to 15–20 cm (6–8 in) are dark green on top usually and violet on the underside. The branched, upright inflorescence, slightly arched at the tip, grows 60–80 cm (24–32 in) and carries

Oncidium gardneri (1/2 nat. size)

numerous flowers, each 5 cm (2 in) across. The egg-shaped sepals are brown with yellow horizontal bars towards the edge. The central sepal is concave and the two lateral sepals are fused together for almost half their length. The relatively large petals are broadly oval with an undulating rim and connected by means of a short bridge. They are brown with yellow marbling around the edge. The lip, which is bridged to the flower, is fan-shaped with an undulating edge, carrying at its base two small lobes. It is golden yellow with red-brown mottling, both around the base and (rather less pronounced) around the rim. The fleshy, triangular callus carries small red warts at the front and at the tip two further wart-like protuberances.
Habitat Brazil.
Flowering season Summer.

Oncidium krameranum
Characteristics Named after the Hamburg nursery gardener Kramer, this species has some-what compressed, nearly circular and closely arranged pseudobulbs, 2.5–4 cm (1–1½ in) long. The individual leaves, 15–20 cm (2–6 in) long and

Oncidium krameranum (× 1.4)

approximately 7 cm (2¾ in) wide, are rather leathery, elongated elliptical and pointed. They are dark green with faint brownish violet mottling. The slim, erect and 60–90 cm (24–36 in) long flower stem has distinct nodes at intervals and bears solitary flowers, growing in succession for several years, so that the stem must not be cut off. The long-lasting, 10–12 cm (4–4¾ in) flowers look like butterflies, in particular the dorsal sepal and the two petals, which are up to 8 cm (3 in) long and very narrow, widen towards the tip and point upwards so as to resemble the antennae of a butterfly. These parts of the flower are red-brown, yellow at the undulated edge, with faint yellow markings towards the tip. The two lateral, elongated elliptical sepals curve downwards in a sickle-shape, hugging the front lobe of the lip, have very pronounced undulations around the edge and are mottled red-brown and yellow. The tri-lobed lip has at its base two small, ear-shaped and red-brown and yellow speckled side lobes, with a large kidney-shaped front lobe which is connected by a short, narrow bridge. It has a heavily ruffled margin. The front lobe is light yellow in the centre with a band of light brown or red-brown marbling around the edge. In the lip base is the callus, its five horns clearly visible, speckled yellow and brown. This species is very similar to *O. papilio* (*papilio* = butterfly) as regards habit and flowers, and can only be distinguished by the following charac-

teristics: the pseudobulbs are oval and a little larger (4–5 cm ($1\frac{1}{2}$–2 in) high); the leaves are a fraction longer, but are clearly variegated brown-red; the flower spike is more slender at the top and longer (up to 1.5 m (5 ft)); the central sepal and the petals are a little longer (up to 12 cm ($4\frac{3}{4}$ in)).
Habitat   Ecuador, Colombia; 300–900 m (1000–3000 ft).
Flowering season Late summer, autumn.

Oncidium nubigenum
Characteristics   The egg-shaped, flattish pseudobulbs grow closely together, are 4–6 cm ($1\frac{1}{2}$–$2\frac{1}{2}$ in) long and carry one to two strap-shaped, pointed leaves, folded at the base and about 15 cm (6 in) long. The slender flower stem, up to 50 cm (20 in) long, stands erect or is arched and carries six to twelve flowers like a cloud (= *nubigenum*), 3 cm ($1\frac{1}{4}$ in) in size in panicles, occasionally on more than one branch. The sepals and petals are usually

Oncidium nubigenum (× 2)

greenish dark brown to dark violet-red and sometimes have a very narrow margin of lighter colouring. The lateral sepals are joined, separating only at the tip into two horns and are hidden by the lip. The tri-lobed lip consists of two small roundish side lobes, joined immediately without a clearly defined bridge to the front lobe, which is large, of a broad kidney-shape, and slightly undulated around the edge. The entire lip has a white to pink colour with strong violet speckles. Between the two side lobes is a yellow callus. A very similar species with nearly the same distribution is *O. cucullatum* which is a little larger and has more elongated flowers (with a narrower kidney-shape front lobe, joined by a more defined, narrow bridge and carrying random violet spots). The species described is sometimes considered as *O. cucullatum* var. *nubigenum*.

Habitat Ecuador; at altitudes of 2500 – 4000 m (8320 – 13320 ft).

Flowering season Autumn, winter.

Oncidium ornithorhynchum

Characteristics This widely-grown popular species has closely arranged, egg-shaped and slightly compressed pseudobulbs, 5–8 cm (2–3 in) long and enclosed by sheaths. The 25–30 cm (10–12 in) long and about 4 cm (1½ in) wide leaves, usually in pairs, are lanceolate and not very robust. There are normally two inflorescences to a new shoot which appear at the two narrower sides of the pseudobulbs, are protected by the sheaths and grow up to 60 cm (24 in), but usually less. The numerous flowers are carried in panicles on arched, branching spikes. The 2 cm (¾ in) flowers, lasting around four weeks, have a beautiful, light-violet to rose-red colouring and exude a heavy vanilla-like scent. The callus is golden yellow. The sepals and petals are both around 1 cm (⅜ in) long and are tongue-shaped, narrowing towards the base. The dorsal sepal is recurved. At the base of the violin-shaped lip is the callus with five parallel combs and two small, horn-like extensions. The anther is beak-shaped (= *ornithorhynchum*).

Habitat Mexico to Costa Rica; at altitudes of approximately 1500 m (5000 ft).

Flowering season Autumn, winter.

Oncidium pusillum
syn. *Psygmorchis pusilla*

Characteristics This tiny (= *pusillum*), pseudobulbless *Oncidium* species has 3–6 cm (1¼–2½ in) lanceolate leaves, in fan formation, similar to irises, but bent slightly in a sickle-shape. Between the leaves grow one to six individual flowers per each fan formation, which only just rise above the leaves. As in the case of *O. krameranum*, new flowers appear successively on the same flower stem. The relatively large flowers grow approximately 2.5 cm (1 in) long and 2 cm (¾ in) wide. The tongue-shaped, yellow sepals grow only to about 5 mm (³⁄₁₆ in); the petals are of the same size and yellow, marked brownish red. The lateral sepals are hidden by the striking lip. The tri-lobed lip has two brilliant yellow, ear-shaped side lobes which are connected with the lip base by short bridges, and a kidney-shaped, incised front lobe, which is also brilliant yellow. The lip base has also red-

Oncidium ornithorhynchum (nat. size)

Oncidium pusillum (× 1.8)

orange marbling around the white, red-orange spotted callus.

Habitat Mexico, Trinidad to Brazil and Bolivia.

Flowering season Usually throughout the year.

Oncidium triquetrum

Characteristics This pseudobulbless species has four or more plicate, pointed, fleshy leaves of triangular (= *triquetrum*) cross-section, growing to a length of 8–15 cm (3–6 in) and about 1.5 cm ($\frac{1}{2}$ in) wide; one of the sides has a groove. The slim flower stem, up to 20 cm (8 in) long, appears from the foot of the leaves, carries a cluster of five to 15 flowers and usually forms in subsequent years further side stems. The long-lasting 2.5 cm (1 in) flowers have lanceolate, red-brown to greenish-violet and white-rimmed sepals of which the lateral sepals are joined together and obscured by the lip. The oval and pointed petals are white with red-brown colouring along the central axis. The 1.5 cm ($\frac{1}{2}$ in) long lip has ear-shaped side-lobes, which are slightly up-turned, a heart-shaped to oval central lobe and at the base a yellow callus. The lip colour is red-brown dotted with white and with a pure white area around the edge.

Habitat Jamaica.

Flowering season Usually summer.

Oncidium variegatum

Characteristics The rhizome forms offshoots, which can branch out and along which arise at intervals the pseudobulbless, iris-shaped leaf tufts. These consist of four to six rigid, pointed and slightly recurving leaves which grow 4–7 cm ($1\frac{1}{2}$–$2\frac{3}{4}$ in) long and are toothed around the edge. The flower stem is nearly 30 cm (12 in) long and carries towards the tip six to twelve long-lasting flowers, approximately 2 cm ($\frac{3}{4}$ in) in diameter. The egg-shaped, concave central sepal points upwards, whereas the lateral sepals fuse together for nearly their full length and are hidden behind the lip. The tongue-shaped, undulated petals spread sideways. Both sepals and petals are white, variegated

Oncidium triquetrum (× 2.5)

Oncidium variegatum (× 3.5)

ing sepals and petals are rather similar. The broad, rounded lip lobe is connected with the other parts of the flower by a narrow bridge and has a small callus at its base. The column is slender and slightly curved.

Cultivation The dainty *Sigmatostalix* species are best cultivated in small pots with good drainage or in wooden baskets. Compost is a mixture of osmunda or tree fern fibre with chopped sphagnum. The species with creeping rhizomes can also be cultivated on bark with a little compost or pieces of tree-fern. As the leaves are delicate, they should not be exposed to direct sunlight, although they tolerate plenty of light. During the growing period in spring and summer regular and plentiful water should be given so as to avoid shrinking and drying out of the pseudobulbs. A rest period of two to three weeks is advisable before the pseudobulbs are fully matured for ripening and to encourage flowering purposes. After this, regular watering should be resumed, as no real rest period is required. *Sigmatostalix* species require intermediate conditions and a sufficiently moist atmosphere. They are extremely free-flowering and relatively easily cultivated.

Sigmatostalix radicans
syn. *Ornithophora radicans*

Characteristics On slim, creeping rhizomes bearing many roots (*radicans* = rooting) form at 2 cm ($\frac{3}{4}$ in) intervals narrow egg-shaped, 3–5 cm ($1\frac{1}{4}$–2 in) high pseudobulbs which carry two leaves at the apex and are enclosed at their base by leaf-like sheaths. The leaves are narrow and grass-like, reaching 10–15 cm (4–6 in), and no more than 0.5 cm ($\frac{1}{8}$ in) wide. Between the sheaths at the foot of the pseudobulbs issue the inflorescences, which are usually arching and grow a little longer than the leaves. The six to twelve widely spaced, scented and interestingly structured flowers are about 1 cm ($\frac{3}{8}$ in) in diameter. The lanceolate, greenish sepals and petals are recurved and grow around 5 mm ($\frac{3}{16}$ in) long. The white, broadly oval lip is connected by a yellow bridge and has to each side of the bridge a white appendage which stands erect. The fleshy bridge carries a spherical callosity and a nose-shaped extension. The column protrudes like a stem and is dark-violet, ending at the apex in beak-shaped, yellow anthers.

(= *variegatum*) with reddish brown and yellow towards the base. The lip is tri-lobed. The two side lobes are toothed around the edge and have an elongated oval shape. The kidney-shaped, undulated and pure white front lobe connects to the rest of the lip via a narrow, very short bridge. Between the side lobes is the reddish brown and yellow patterned callus. The column has at the front two small, ear-shaped appendages, toothed around the edge.

Habitat Florida, West Indies.

Flowering season Winter, spring.

Sigmatostalix

Tr. Oncidieae Subtr. Oncidiinae

Etymology *Sigma* = Greek letter; *stalix* = pole; referring to its sigma-shaped column.

Description There are around twelve known species in this genus and they are all epiphytes, found in South America in the area between Mexico and Brazil. They can all be classified as small orchids, and are much liked by growers because of their multifloral habit and very interestingly shaped flowers. The flat and narrow pseudobulbs carry at the apex one or two linear, sometimes grass-like leaves and are enclosed by linear sheaths. The flowers form abundantly and in panicles from the base of the pseudobulbs, protected by the sheaths. The star-shaped, radiat-

Sigmatostalix radicans (× 6)

Habitat Brazil.
Flowering season Autumn, winter.

Trichocentrum

Tr. Oncidieae Subtr. Trichocentrinae
Etymology From *thrix, trichos* (Gr.) = hair;
centron = spur; referring to its long, thin spur.
Description This genus is distributed throughout tropical America from Mexico to Brazil and
comprises approximately twenty, mainly epiphytic species. The pseudobulbs are usually small
and barely visible because they are hidden by their
surrounding leaf-like sheaths. The relatively large,
handsome flowers normally appear singly on short
stems. Whereas the sepals and petals in star-
shaped formation look rather similar, the spurred
lip contrasts very strongly in both size and colour.
The short column carries at its tip on both sides a
toothed, ear-shaped appendage.
Cultivation Although *Trichocentrum* species
look attractive, are relatively easily cultivated and
are not ultrasensitive to errors of cultivation, they
are nevertheless little represented in orchid collections. This dwarf, epiphytic plant is cultivated

either in small pots with good drainage or on bark
or pieces of tree-fern. Compost is the usual mixture of sphagnum moss and osmunda or tree fern
fibre, although sphagnum can be dispensed with.
Trichocentrum species are best kept under intermediate conditions. As they have no defined rest
period, they must be watered regularly and ad-
equately without however fully saturating the
compost, which would lead to rotting. The environment of the plants should be airy, yet maintain a rather high humidity. They tolerate plenty of
light, but excessive sun should be avoided so that
the leaves do not scorch. Because of their slow
growth, they need repotting very infrequently.
They are very sensitive to being disturbed by
repotting.

Trichocentrum tigrinum
Characteristics In habit this species is typical of
the genus, only the leaves are mottled red and the
ends are blunted. The flowers have a diameter of
approximately 5–6 cm (2–2½ in). The narrow,
tongue-shaped and slightly pointed sepals and
petals are coloured greenish yellow and carry
brown flecks in varying densities

Trichocentrum tigrinum (× 2)

(*tigrinum* = tigerish). The broadly oval, bi-lobed lip is slightly undulated around the edge, and in colour is white, apart from a brilliant yellow patch at the base surrounding three combs on either side of which it is violet-red. The blunted spur is very short. The short column is yellowish with violet-red markings; at the tip is a prominent light yellow anther.

Habitat Ecuador.

Flowering season Summer, autumn.

Trichopilia

Tr. Oncidieae Subtr. Trichopiliinae

Etymology *Thrix, trichos* (Gr.) = hair; *pilion* = cap; referring to the tufts of hair around the upper rim of the column.

Description This genus comprises approximately fifteen species, mostly epiphytic and found only in the tropical forests of America from Mexico and Cuba to Brazil. The flattened, roughly oval pseudobulbs are enclosed by sheaths and carry a single, leathery leaf. From the base of the pseudobulbs develop pendulous inflorescences with one to five (rarely up to eight) rather large and fascinating flowers. With their radially spread sepals and petals and their trumpet- to tube-like lip enclosing the column, they have a strong resemblance to cattleya flowers. Many of the species have delightfully fragrant flowers.

Cultivation *Trichopilia* are relatively easily cultivated under intermediate conditions, although they tolerate a cool place during winter. They are planted in pots with good drainage, or better still in wooden baskets, as their flowers are usually pendulous. Compost is the usual mixture for epiphytes (osmunda fibre and sphagnum moss, but with rather less sphagnum). During the summer growing period the roots require plenty of moisture and copious watering is essential. After the pseudobulbs have finished growing, they need

Trichopilia suavis (2/3 nat. size)

a rest period of several weeks with very little watering so as to avoid continued vegetative growth and to encourage flowering. Because of their natural habitat, trichopilias require an airy and shady site with sufficient humidity. During their winter rest period, little watering is required. Many *Trichopilia* species are more easily brought to flower if the plants are divided regularly. Division should be carried out at the same time as repotting, every three to four years. When planting, care must be taken to ensure there is enough room at the foot of the pseudobulbs for the flowers to grow.

Trichopilia suavis

Characteristics This delightful (= *suavis*) and most beautiful species has flat, oval to round, grey-green pseudobulbs which are enclosed at the base by paper-like sheaths and grow up to 7 cm ($2\frac{3}{4}$ in) long. The elliptical lanceolate, leathery leaves are borne on a short stem and reach 10–30 cm (4–12 in) in length and 3–6 cm ($1\frac{1}{4}$–$2\frac{1}{2}$ in) in width. The short, slightly pendulous flower stem carries two to five superbly scented flowers about 10 cm (4 in) in diameter. The lanceolate sepals and petals usually have wavy edges; their colour is white to creamy, sometimes with pale pink speckles. The large, cone-shaped white to cream lip broadens outwards and has strong violet-pink speckling; the front rim is ruffled all round. In the throat of the lip is a large, brownish yellow patch which covers and surrounds a striking keel.

Habitat Costa Rica to Colombia; at altitudes of approximately 1800–2500 m (6000–8320 ft).

Flowering season Spring.

Promenaea

Tr. Oncidieae Subtr. Zygopetalinae

Etymology Named after the Greek priestess Promeneia.

Description This genus covers approximately ten dwarf-growing species which are primarily epiphytes and found at lower altitudes in Brazil. *Promenaea* species have small, flat pseudobulbs of broadly oval shape, which usually carry two elongated elliptical leaves. The relatively large flowers are colourful and form singly or in pairs on a short, pendulous stem. Petals and sepals look rather similar. The lip is tri-lobed, with the two small side lobes standing almost vertically.

Cultivation As in their natural surroundings, *Promenaea* species require intermediate to warm conditions with relatively high humidity. They are best cared for in small hanging pots with good drainage or in wooden baskets, as the flowers are pendulous. Compost is the usual mixture of osmunda fibre and sphagnum moss. During the growing period they should be generously watered. The rest period commences after flowering, when watering must be reduced, without however allowing the plant to dry out as this would be harmful. A light situation without direct sunshine is recommended so as to avoid scorching the leaves. The roots do not tolerate old compost which can stagnate with repeated saturation so that repotting should be carried out with completely new compost every two to three years.

Promenaea stapelioides
Characteristics The roundish, laterally compressed pseudobulbs are approximately 2 cm ($\frac{3}{4}$ in) in diameter and enveloped by two leaf-like sheaths; they carry usually two tongue-shaped, about 5 cm (2 in) long leaves. The one to two flowers, 4–5 cm ($1\frac{1}{2}$–2 in) in diameter, spring from the side of the pseudobulbs and are of similar appearance to the succulent *Stapelia* species (= *stapelioides*). (The stapelias are not orchids; their common name is carrion flower.) The pointed sepals and petals are a broad oval in shape, slightly overlapping, and turning downwards a little. Against a yellowish-green ground they have a dense covering of dark violet ripples. The tri-lobed lip has narrow, elongated side lobes which protrude and are speckled yellow and dark violet, and a nearly circular front lobe, mottled dark violet with a lighter colouring towards the rim. The column is greenish to pale yellow.
Habitat Brazil.
Flowering season Summer, autumn.

Zygopetalum
Tr. Oncidieae Subtr. Zygopetalinae
Etymology From *zygon* (Gr.) = yoke, *petalon* = petal; referring to the fusing of sepals and petals with the base of the column.
Description The genus *Zygopetalum* contains around 20 species, some terrestrial, some epiphytic and others lithophytic. Their distribution area is tropical Central and South America with the focal point in Brazil. Most species have large, ellipsoidal pseudobulbs with two or more leaves. The erect or slightly arched flower stem appears with the young lead and bears in loose arrangement several handsome flowers. The petals and sepals look similar and spread out in star form-

ation. The lip has a large, fan-shaped central lobe and sometimes small side lobes. The distinguishing feature of this genus is the manner in which the lip clearly forms a short chin jointed to the base of the column.
Cultivation Although some *Zygopetalum* species are terrestrial in their natural habitat, all can be cultivated in the usual compost for epiphytes. The mixture of osmunda fibre and a little sphagnum moss can however be supplemented with some beech leaves and a little garden soil. So as to obtain good drainage in the pot, it should be about one-third filled with broken crocks. Some species, e.g. *Z. maxillare*, also grow very well on pieces of tree-fern. During their growing period in summer, the zygopetalums require much humidity. The air must be kept moist and fresh. They should be placed in a fairly shady position under intermediate conditions. During the rest period watering should be reduced to a level sufficient to prevent the pseudobulbs and leaves from shrivelling.

Zygopetalum intermedium
Characteristics This type is often mistaken for *Z. mackayi* (*intermedium* = in between), to which it has close similarities. The closely arranged pseudobulbs are usually of a broad egg-shape and grow to a height of about 9 cm ($3\frac{1}{2}$ in) and a diameter of 5 cm (2 in). They become wrinkled with increasing age. The three to five rather fleshy leaves growing from the apex of the pseudobulb are strap-shaped to lanceolate, reducing towards the base, being up to 45 cm (18 in) long and about 6 cm ($2\frac{1}{2}$ in) wide. The straight flower spike, about 60 cm (24 in) long, appears from the axil of the sheaths enveloping the base of the pseudobulbs and is itself provided with numerous bracts. The wax-like, pleasantly aromatic and long-lasting flowers (four to seven per flower spike) are 7–8 cm ($2\frac{3}{4}$–3 in) in size and open nearly simultaneously. The elongated elliptical sepals and petals are yellowish green with reddish brown markings. The slightly crinkled, fan-shaped and rounded lip is white with small longitudinal violet flecks in a radial arrangement from the base. The distinguishing features between this species and *Z. mackayi* are: the petals are as long as the dorsal sepal (unlike *Z. mackayi*, where they are considerably shorter); the central

Zygopetalum intermedium (nat. size)

Aërangis rhodosticta (× 1.8)

part of the lip is covered with hairs; the lower surface of the column is hairy (and not smooth); the bracts are rather short.

Habitat Brazil, Peru.

Flowering season Autumn, winter.

Aërangis

Tr. Vandeae Subtr. Aërangidinae

Etymology From (Gr.) *aër* = air; *angos* = receptacle; referring to its growing 'in the air'.

Description This genus comprises a little over 70 species, usually diminutive and short-stemmed, growing primarily epiphytically in tropical Africa, Madagascar and neighbouring islands. Botanists consider them to be distinct from the genus *Angraecum*, because of the differences in flower structure and form.

Cultivation Care is basically as for *Angraecum*. During the rest period after flowering less watering is required and the temperature needs to be lowered a little. During winter an intermediate position is sufficient, whereas a warm spot is advantageous during summer.

Aërangis luteo-alba var. **rhodosticta**

Characteristics The short flower stem is usually pendulous. The light green, strap-shaped leaves, slightly falcate, grow up to 15 cm (6 in) long and are unevenly bi-lobed at the tip. The usually pendulous inflorescence is up to 35 cm (14 in) long with six to twenty-five flowers. The almost flat, fairly long-lasting flowers form two parallel rows on the same plane and are about 3 cm (1¼ in) in diameter. The nearly round sepals and petals are slightly recurved and are either pure white or white tinged with green or yellow. The column is a brilliant red and forms the focal point of the flower (*rhodosticta* = rose-red point).

Habitat Central Africa (Cameroon to Ethiopia and Tanzania).

Flowering season Autumn to spring.

Angraecum

Tr. Vandeae Subtr. Angraecinae

Etymology The Malayan name *angrek* means an epiphytic orchid.

Description The genus *Angraecum* is found in Africa and contains nearly 200 species, although only a few are cultivated. Faced with so many species, a botanical demarcation is difficult. However, generally it can be said that they all have monopodial growth with usually smooth, fleshy leaves. The white or greenish flowers have a spur.

Cultivation *Angraecum* species are best cultivated in meshed baskets, in pots with holes or on cork bark or pieces of tree-fern which should be suspended near a window. Most species prefer full light or at least semi-shade. Compost is osmunda with chopped tree-fern or a mixture of this with chopped sphagnum moss. Repotting is required only every three to four years in spring. All species require plenty of fresh, circulating air, which should be very warm in summer and always moist.

Angraecum eburneum

Characteristics The very strong, densely leaved stem can reach up to 1 m (3¼ ft). The leathery, dark green leaves grow 30–50 cm (12–20 in) long and about 5 cm (2 in) wide; they are unevenly bi-lobed at their tip and spread horizontally or hang slightly. It is usual for several inflorescences, with dense flower clusters, to appear simultaneously; they grow to the same length as the leaves, either

Angraecum eburneum (nat. size)

upright or at an angle. The wax-like, long-lasting, pleasantly scented flowers are about 6 cm (2½ in) in size, arranged in two rows, back to back. The radiating, tongue-shaped sepals and petals are greenish-white. The lip is erect; it is nearly round or of a broad egg-shape and ivory-coloured (= *eburneum*) with a green suffusion towards the throat. The lip ends in a short, sharp point with a narrow ridge from there stretching to the calyx. The thin, green spur is up to 10 cm (4 in) long.
Habitat Madagascar.
Flowering season Late autumn, winter.

Angraecum leonis
Characteristics This almost stemless plant carries only a few, rather fleshy leaves, which are 12–25 cm (4¾–10 in) long, arching in the form of a sickle and sprouting close together vertically from the stem. The strong inflorescence, borne upwards at an angle, carries three to six short-stemmed, long-lasting and scented flowers, about 7 cm (2¾ in) across. The lanceolate, pointed and reflexed petals and sepals are white to yellowish and about 4 cm (1½ in) long. The petals are a little broader than the sepals. The shape of the lip resembles a sea-shell, is

Angraecum leonis (3/4 nat. size)

about 4 cm (1½ in) long, white and ends in a small, pointed lobe, and continues backwards into a greenish, 15 cm (6 in) spur in the shape of a questionmark.
Habitat Madagascar, Comoro Islands.
Flowering season Winter.

Angraecum sesquipedale
Characteristics The strong stem, woody below and densely leaved above, reaches about 1 m (3¼ ft) and is covered with strong roots. The bluish-green, leathery and strap-shaped leaves, up to 30 cm (12 in) long and 4–5 cm (1½–2 in) wide, are arranged in two rows. The inflorescence forms horizontally and is slightly pendulous; it is about the same length as the leaves, and carries on its stem brownish bracts and at the apex two to four wax-like, scented flowers of a beautiful ivory colour. The flowers last approximately three to four weeks, and are 12–15 cm (4¾–6 in) across, excluding the spur. The petals and sepals constitute a six-pointed star, hence the name given to it in its country of origin—star of Madagascar. Sepals and petals are broad at the base, narrowing towards the apex. The lip is slightly broader and also has a long triangular shape, slightly enveloping the column, with the side rims turned upwards at the tip. At the foot of the lip, underneath the short and thick column, is a small longitudinal callus. The yellowish green, thread-like lip spur hangs down to an astonishing length of around 45 cm (18 in) (*sesquipedale* = 1½ ft long) and is slightly recurved towards the end. The nectar is at the base of the spur and can be reached only by a moth with a proboscis of appropriate length. Charles Darwin predicted in 1862 the existence of such a pollinator, which was however discovered only as late as 1903 and named *Xanthopan morgani* var. *praedicta* (= predicted).
Habitat Madagascar; at altitudes of up to 100 m (330 ft).
Flowering season Usually winter.

Ascocentrum
Tr. Vandeae Subtr. Ascocentrinae
Etymology From (Gr.) *askos* = hose; *kentron* = spur; referring to the hose-like spur of the flower.
Description Of the nine species known at

Angraecum sesquipedale (nat. size)

Ascocentrum miniatum (× 1.2)

present, perhaps six are cultivated, although usually under the previous name of *Saccolabium*. All species are short-stemmed, small, densely leaved, monopodial epiphytes. The linear leaves have closely toothed edges, similar to the *Vanda* genus. The flowers are borne in clusters on short, upright stems. The blooms last a long time and are very effective with their strong colouring.

Cultivation *Ascocentrum* species require as much light as possible, although scorching of the leaves through excessive sun must be avoided. Under the right conditions the leaves grow closely together, are robust, long-lasting and yellowish green. If there is insufficient light, then the leaves become dark green and are much too long, too far apart and do not overlap on the stalk. The leaves look better like this, but the plants will not flower. *Ascocentrum* species prefer warm humid surroundings with fresh, freely circulating air, particularly in the summer period of active growth. On hot days the compost, roots and leaves can be syringed. The plants require copious watering, although care must be taken to ensure that the roots are not subjected to continued sogginess. It is furthermore important that no water remains on the sensitive, growing tip of the stem, otherwise rot may set in. The compost poses no particular problems. The most varied mixtures are used. For example, it could be a mixture of osmunda fibre and sphagnum moss with a few pieces of charcoal; the all-important thing is good drainage. The plants can be planted in meshed baskets or pots. Yearly repotting is not necessary; a renewal of the compost on the surface is sufficient. Propagation can be carried out during repotting by separating the young root-bearing shoots or by division of the stem at the point where the roots start to form.

Ascocentrum miniatum
Characteristics The rather thick and woody stalk is usually less than 10 cm (4 in) long and hidden behind stipules. The very fleshy and fairly straight leaves are 8–15 cm (3–6 in) long and about 2 cm ($\frac{3}{4}$ in) wide. At their base they are very heavily folded and the tips are asymmetrical, being either unevenly blunted or bi-lobed. The flowers are closely clustered together in an erect column up to 13 cm (5 in) tall. The flowers are about 2 cm ($\frac{3}{4}$ in) in size and vary greatly in their colouring, from orange to flame-red to vermilion ($=miniatum$). Sepals and petals are elliptical, blunt and spreading. The lip is only about 7 mm ($\frac{1}{4}$ in), with small, vertical, triangular side lobes and a tongue-shaped front lobe. The cylindrical, blunt spur is narrower at the upper end and nearly as long as the sepals. The column is very short with a violet anther.

Habitat Himalayas to Malayan Peninsula, Java and Borneo.

Flowering season Spring.

Gastrochilus
Tr. Vandeae Subtr. Saccolabiinae

Etymology From *gaster* (Gr.) = belly; *cheilos* = lip; referring to its belly-shaped lip.

Description This genus comprises approximately fifteen epiphytic species which were formerly classified under the *Saccolabium* genus. Even today many orchid catalogues list them under their old name. The distribution area of *Gastrochilus* species extends from India via Indochina to Taiwan and Indonesia. All species have monopodial growth and most of them are of compact size with few, leathery leaves. Several relatively large, handsome and interesting flowers form on a shortish stem. The elongated, rounded and spreading petals and sepals are very similar to each other and almost form a semi-circle. The lip consists of a belly- or slipper-shaped rear part opening out into a disc-shaped front part, which is more prominent in some species than in others and is fringed around the edge. The belly-shaped part of the lip merges into the very short column. The hood-shaped anther carries two pollinia on short stems.

Cultivation Depending on their habitat, *Gastrochilus* species require intermediate to warm conditions. During the growing season in summer they require plenty of water and humidity. Sufficient air circulation must be ensured. During the rather indefinite rest period in winter they require less watering, but they must not be neglected, as they do not have any pseudobulbs. Light syringing from time to time prevents drying out. To encourage flowering, a light, but not too sunny place is recommended. Compost is a mixture of osmunda or tree-fern fibre and sphagnum moss. Dwarf varieties are best planted on cork bark or in baskets, which show up their short-stemmed inflorescences to better effect. Propagation is possible by cuttings, removing shoots from plants after they have stopped growing in the same way as for *Aërides* species.

Gastrochilus calceolaris
syn. *Saccolabium calceolare*

Characteristics Each short stalk carries four to six tongue-shaped, unevenly bi-lobed leathery leaves, about 15 cm (6 in) long and 2 cm ($\frac{3}{4}$ in) wide. The paniculate inflorescence is borne on a strong, 2–5 cm ($\frac{3}{4}$–2 in) flower stem. The flowers, six to twelve in number and about 2 cm ($\frac{3}{4}$ in) across, stand close together, last a long time, and are slightly scented. The greenish to yellowish or light brown sepals and petals have a varying number of brown to purple spots and sometimes turn slightly forwards. The slipper-shaped (= *calceolaris*) lip sac is smaller than that of other *Gastrochilus* species and is yellow with reddish to brownish specks.

The front lobe of the lip is covered with down, is semi-circular and basically white with an orange centre and red-brown spots, fringed around the edge. The column is purple.

Habitat Himalayan region, Burma to Sumatra and Java; in mountain regions.
Flowering season Varying, usually spring.

Gastrochilus dasypogon
syn. *Saccolabium dasypogon*

Characteristics On a short stalk form six to eight leaves, 10–15 cm (4–6 in) long and 3 cm ($1\frac{1}{4}$ in) wide, which are unevenly bi-lobed at their apex. The short, strong flower stem appears between the leaves and carries five to ten flowers which form a circular inflorescence, with their lips all pointing towards the centre. The approximately 2.5 cm (1 in), strongly scented flowers, lasting for around four weeks, have pale yellow, tongue-shaped sepals and petals, which are finely speckled brownish violet, and a white, yellow and red lip. The sac-shaped part of the lip is whitish to yellow at its base with faint violet dots and violet markings around the edge. The flat, semi-circular front lobe is white with a yellow centre and violet spots all over; the edge is fringed like a rough beard (= *dasypogon*).
Habitat Himalaya region to Thailand.
Flowering season Usually autumn.

Gastrochilus calceolaris (× 3.5)

Gastrochilus dasypogon (4/5 nat. size)

Haraëlla

Tr. Vandeae Subtr. Saccolabiinae

Etymology Named after Yoshie Hara of the Taishoku Imperial University in Taiwan, who discovered this genus.

Description There are only two known species in this genus, both of which are found only in Taiwan (Formosa). They are epiphytes with monopodial growth. Orchid collections in Europe and the USA have up to now only the species described below.

Cultivation Being a tropical plant from lower mountain regions, *Haraëlla* species require warm conditions and a relatively high humidity. They need a shady place without direct sunshine. This means that they can be conveniently cultivated together with those *Paphiopedilum* species with tesselated leaves. They can be planted in small pots with a well drained compost (mixture of osmunda or tree-fern fibre and a little sphagnum moss) or better still on tree-fern slabs where their fine roots can spread more readily. They have no rest period so that regular watering is necessary.

Haraëlla retrocalla
syn. *Haraëlla odorata*

Characteristics This magnificent small orchid has closely arranged, leathery, elongated and pointed falcate leaves, 3–4 cm ($1\frac{1}{4}$–$1\frac{1}{2}$ in) long and up to 1 cm ($\frac{3}{8}$ in) wide and borne on a 1 cm ($\frac{3}{8}$ in) stalk. The relatively large flowers appear singly or occasionally in pairs on a 3–4 cm ($1\frac{1}{4}$–$1\frac{1}{2}$ in) long flower stem which grows from the lower part of the leaf stalk. The fleshy, elliptical and approximately 8 mm ($\frac{5}{16}$ in) long sepals and petals are arranged in a semicircle and are pale yellow. The petals are 3 mm ($\frac{1}{8}$ in) wide and narrower than the sepals which are 4 mm ($\frac{5}{32}$ in) wide. The oval, tri-lobed lip is nearly 1.5 cm ($\frac{1}{2}$ in) long and 1 cm ($\frac{3}{8}$ in) wide. The two roundish, rather delicate side lobes stand upwards at an angle. The large central lobe is finely fringed around the edge and slightly recurved. The lip has a pale yellow band around the edge; the remaining parts are dark purple, sparsely covered with hairs and have an inner triangular, fleshy callus (= *retrocalla*). The spherical column, about 2.5 mm ($\frac{1}{16}$ in) in size, is yellow.

Haraëlla retrocalla (× 3)

Habitat   Taiwan; at altitudes of 300–1000 m (1000–3330 ft).
Flowering season   Usually summer to autumn (also often more than once during the year).

Aërides

Tr. Vandeae Subtr. Sarochilinae
Etymology   From *aër* (Gr.) = air; grows 'in the air'.
Description   This genus covers around 60 species, most of which are pendulous monopodial epiphytes. Most species reach a height of 1 m (3¼ ft) and over. The leaves are thick, leathery and arching. The roots do not like to bury themselves in the compost, as they are true aerial roots. The wax-like, pleasantly scented flowers form in cylindrically pendulous spikes of varying density, which develop from the axils of the central leaves on the stem. Most flowers open together and are long-lasting.
Cultivation   *Aërides* species are best planted in meshed baskets, in pots with holes, or on cork bark where they have enough room for their exposed

roots, as these do not tolerate stagnant conditions. The compost should furthermore be fairly loose and well ventilated (mixture of osmunda or tree-fern fibre and a little sphagnum). Repotting should be undertaken as rarely as possible, as the roots break easily. *Aërides* species require at all times warm (during the summer heat 30–35°C (85–95°F) would not be excessive), humid and airy conditions. An exception is *A. japonica*, which grows under cool to intermediate conditions, and *A. fieldingii*, which grows under intermediate conditions in the Himalaya region. A light situation is required to assist flowering. The leathery leaves will tolerate direct sunshine for a short time. *Aërides* species have no definite rest period. During the winter, when growth slows down, an intermediate, but not too dry spot is sufficient. Many fully-grown plants develop growths, which can be removed and potted after they have reached a sufficient size and have formed two to three roots of their own.

Aërides fieldingii
Characteristics   Named after Colonel Fielding, this species has a short stem, densely covered with

Aërides fieldingii (5/6 nat. size)

foliage. Whilst the lower leaves are pendulous, the upper leaves stand upright or are slightly arched; they grow to a length of 20–25 cm (8–10 in) and a width of about 4 cm ($1\frac{1}{2}$ in). The pendulous flower spike is up to 50 cm (20 in) long containing 25 to 30 or more clustered flowers, each 2.5–3.5 cm (1–$1\frac{3}{8}$ in) in diameter. The wax-like and scented flowers are white, shaded with palish violet or are spotted, particularly towards the margins. The central sepals and petals are an inverted egg-shape and the two lateral sepals have a broadly oval shape. The triangular to trapeziform lip is white at the edge and merges into a strong violet-red towards its base. At the base it has two small, rolled-up side lobes, which hide the opening of a short, funnel-shaped spur.

Habitat Himalaya region (Sikkim, Assam).
Flowering season Late spring.

Aërides maculosa

Characteristics The leathery leaves grow 15–22 cm (6–$8\frac{3}{4}$ in) long and up to 5 cm (2 in) wide. The dense, branched inflorescences are somewhat longer than the leaves and overhang them. The flowers are approximately 3.5 cm ($1\frac{3}{8}$ in) in size. The oval, blunt and about 1.5 cm ($\frac{1}{2}$ in) long sepals and petals are white at the base and elsewhere light red with small, purple spotting (*maculosa* = densely spotted). The lip is almost 2 cm ($\frac{3}{4}$ in) long with two small, whitish side lobes at its base and a large, slightly wavy, egg-shaped, purple front lobe. The horn-like spur is short, 7 mm ($\frac{5}{16}$ in) long, slightly curved downwards with a greenish tinted apex. The column is white with a yellowish anther cap.

Habitat India (particularly Kerala).
Flowering season Early summer.

Phalaenopsis

Tr. Vandeae Subtr. Sarcochilinae
Etymology From *phalaina* (Gr.) = moth; *opsis* = look; referring to the moth-like appearance of the flowers.
Description This genus has monopodial growth with short stems and no pseudobulbs. It comprises about 70 species which are mostly epiphytes growing around forest edges, where they are protected from direct sunshine by the foliage of trees. Their distribution area stretches from India via the Malayan Peninsula and Indonesia to Northern Australia and the Philippines. *Phalaenopsis* species have fleshy, rather wide leaves in two tier

Aërides maculosa (nat. size)

formation, and thick, strong roots; some have short inflorescences and others long, pendulous panicles which issue from underneath the leaves. Characteristic of the usually large, magnificent flowers is the tri-lobed lip, which is connected directly to the foot of the column without a hinge. With many species the front lobe of the lip ends in two antennae. In view of their beautiful flowers and the relative ease of growing, phalaenopses are frequently cultivated. Orchid specialists have produced many wonderful hybrids. As the flower panicles last very well when cut, they are a popular florist's flower.

Cultivation *Phalaenopsis* species are found in the Asiatic tropics at altitudes of 200–400 m (660–1320 ft) only, and therefore require constant warm conditions and permanently moist air. Sufficient air circulation is also desirable. As their leaves are their sole means of storing nutrients, they must never dry out although the compost must be sufficiently porous, so as to avoid stagnant conditions. When watering, care should be taken that no water remains on the apex of the growths, otherwise the new growth might rot, resulting in the death of the entire plant. In summer, during the growth period, regular watering is required,

with frequent syringing so that the humidity is increased. During the rest period in winter watering should be reduced. The plants must be shaded from direct sunlight to avoid leaf scorch. Phalaenopses can be planted in pots or baskets with good drainage or even on cork bark. The most suitable compost is osmunda or tree-fern fibre which can be enriched with some sphagnum moss. Some orchid growers also add bark or prefer a pure bark mixture. When repotting, which becomes necessary only every few years, care must be taken that the base of the plant remains exposed so that the leaves do not rot and new roots can grow more freely. Some species form young plants from the thickening of the flower spikes, giving an easy means of propagation.

Phalaenopsis cornu-cervi
Characteristics The leathery, elongated leaves, few in number and narrowing towards the base, reach a length of 15–25 cm (6–10 in) and a width of about 4 cm (1½ in). The flower stem grows up to 20 cm (8 in), is flattened and widens towards the top. It stands upright at an angle and carries six to twelve wax-like flowers in two rows, similar to deer antlers (*cornu-cervi* = deer antlers), with only one

Phalaenopsis cornu-cervi (× 1.5)

Phalaenopsis esmeralda (× 1.2)

or very few flowers opening at a time. The approximately 5 cm (2 in) flowers last a long time and are slightly scented. Sepals and petals have an elongated, very pointed shape, are very similar to each other and are arranged in a star-shape. The petals are only slightly smaller than the sepals. Sepals and petals have a yellow to greenish-yellow basic colouring with red-brown mottling. The small lip is white to yellow, with erect side lobes and a kidney-shaped front lobe. The column projects forward and is yellow with red-brown spots at the base.

Habitat Malayan Peninsula, Indonesia.
Flowering season Spring, summer.

Phalaenopsis esmeralda

syn. *Doritis pulcherrima, Phalaenopsis buyssoniana*
Characteristics The 10–20 cm (4–8 in) long and about 4 cm (1½ in) wide leaves are elongated elliptical, pointed and leathery. They are dark green, sometimes variegated with brown-violet. The thin, erect flower stems do not branch out, grow to 30–45 cm (12–18 in) and bear fifteen to twenty flowers in loose arrangement. The flowers

can vary greatly in size and colour; their diameter is 2–4 cm (¾–1½ in). The upper sepal and petals look alike, being elongated, oval in shape and spreading. The lateral sepals are broader and usually re-curved. The colour of the sepals and petals ranges from nearly white through pink and light violet to dark violet. The tri-lobed, dark violet lip has erect oval lateral lobes, and an oval to tongue-shaped pink-veined front lobe, which is recurved around the margin. There is a two-pointed callus on the disc.

Habitat Burma, Thailand, Laos to Sumatra.
Flowering season Autumn.

Phalaenopsis violacea

Characteristics The fleshy leaves are broadly oval to elongated elliptical, growing up to 25 cm (10 in) long and around 10 cm (4 in) wide. The strong, 10–12 cm (4–4¾ in) long inflorescence is slightly arching, carries two to five flowers loosely arranged, opening in succession and which are long-lasting. The 5–7 cm (2–2¾ in) flowers have elongated, egg-shaped and pointed sepals and

Phalaenopsis violacea (× 1.5)

petals arranged in star formation. The tri-lobed lip is a little shorter, with convolute golden yellow side lobes and a small, rhomboidal and bare front lobe. The colouring can be classified in two groups, according to habitat. The Bornean species have white to light green sepals and petals which change into a strong violet (= *violacea*) at the base. On the lateral sepals the violet colouring extends over almost the entire half nearest the lip. The front lobe of the lip and the column are also a strong violet. The Malayan species have not such a strong violet colouring, but are pink-violet to a pale crimson; the colour stretching nearly to the tips so that only the tips have a light green tinge. The front lobe of the lip has the same pink-violet colouring.

Habitat Malayan Peninsula, Borneo, Sumatra.
Flowering season Summer, autumn.

Rhynchostylis

Tr. Vandeae Subtr. Sarochilinae
Etymology From *rhygchos* (pronounced rhynchos) (Gr.) = beak; *stylis* = column, pistil; referring to the beak-shaped column.

Description This genus consists of only four species which are in cultivation; they have monopodial growth, a stunted stem, from the base of which shoot the strong roots and from the side of which grows the cylindrical, multiflowered inflorescence. The relatively long leaves are rigidly leathery, unevenly bi-lobed at the apex and caniculate. The entire habit is similar to the genus *Aërides*. The flowers are also very similar, but *Rhynchostylis* flowers can be distinguished from *Aërides* flowers in that the flower spur projects horizontally backwards and stands a little above the undivided lip, which is slightly turned inwards. The distribution area is from India to Thailand and the Philippines.

Cultivation *Rhynchostylis* species are best kept under warm and humid conditions during their growing period in summer. A semi-shady place is advantageous during this period, whereas during the winter rest period they will tolerate a light situation. The temperature can then also be reduced to intermediate, and watering should also be somewhat restricted. They are best planted in a large woven hanging basket, as the flower trusses are usually pendulous. The usual compost for

Rhynchostylis coelestis (× 2.5)

epiphytes will suffice, namely sphagnum moss mixed with osmunda or tree-fern fibre. As the roots are particularly sensitive to repotting, it is advisable to remove the used compost very carefully without removing the plant itself from the wooden basket.

Rhynchostylis coelestis

Characteristics A dense foliage covers the strong stem which grows up to 20 cm (8 in). The strap-shaped leaves reach 10–18 cm (4–7 in) and are about 2 cm ($\frac{3}{4}$ in) wide. They are fleshy and caniculate so that they form a sharp ridge on the underside and overlap at the base. The cylindrical inflorescence has very many closely arranged flowers, stands erect and grows up to 20 cm (8 in) high. The wax-like and scented flowers are approximately 2 cm ($\frac{3}{4}$ in) wide and mainly bluish (*coelestis* = skyblue) in colour, which is an extremely rare colour amongst orchids. The elongated oval sepals and petals radiate outwards, are white at the base, changing to violet-blue towards their apices. The inverted egg-shaped lip is white at the base and otherwise violet-blue. The sac-like spur is laterally very strongly compressed and curves slightly at the tip. The short, beak-shaped column is also blue so that the yellow pollinia stand out prominently.

Habitat Tropical Asia.

Flowering season Summer.

Vanda

Tr. Vandeae Subtr. Vandinae

Etymology Indian name for various vanda orchids.

Description There are around 70 species in this genus, all with monopodial growth and with stems of varying lengths, which are densely covered with leathery leaves. The leaves are mostly strap-shaped, but sometimes terete. The inflorescences grow nearly erect from the leaf axils at the upper part of the plant and carry relatively large, usually scented and strikingly coloured flowers. The shape of the flowers is rather similar for all species. Sepals and petals are usually very similar, spreading radially and narrowing to a point at the base. The tri-lobed lip consists of two small erect side lobes, which normally have a short spur or sac at the base, and a kidney- to violin-shaped central lobe on which are comb-like calli. *Vanda* species are found in tropical Asia, from India and China via Indonesia as far as New Guinea and the Philippines. Being mainly epiphytic orchids, their habitat is on trees and they form strong, long aerial roots with which to find sufficient nutrients and moisture. During recent decades numerous infrageneric and also intergeneric hybrids have been cultivated with related genera, such as for example *Ascocentrum, Aërides* and *Renanthera*, some of which are offered commercially as cut flowers. Multiple cross-hybridization between three, four and more species has also been effected.

Cultivation Many cultivated *Vanda* species, as those described below, require intermediate conditions which can be a little cooler during the rest period. *V. denisoniana* can be placed under intermediate to warm conditions. Many species and in particular most hybrids should be cared for under warm conditions. All species require, however, plenty of light for flowering with slight shading in summer. Given insufficient light and rather too much watering, the leaves will develop beautifully, but grow much too vigorously at the expense of the flowers. During the growth period in summer *Vanda* species require plenty of fresh air with sufficient atmospheric moisture, which is provided by frequent syringing and regular watering. The strong exposed roots absorb the moisture from the air. During the rest period vandas are kept drier, without, however, allowing the leaves to shrivel. When watering, care must always be taken to ensure that no water remains on the apex of the stem, otherwise the new growths will rot. They are best potted in a wooden hanging basket or pot, so that the aerial roots can hang down freely. Good drainage is essential. Compost can be from the most varied mixtures, although the simplest consists of osmunda or tree-fern fibre and a little sphagnum moss, to which can be added a little bark, broken crocks or chopped polystyrene. When repotting in spring (about every three to four years), care must be taken that the stem is not inserted too deeply and is not covered with compost. Generally speaking, most *Vanda* species are relatively easily cared for.

Vanda cristata

Characteristics The strong, densely-leaved stem reaches about 20 cm (8 in) and has numerous roots. The generally horizontal, caniculate leaves, grow 12–15 cm ($4\frac{3}{4}$–6 in) long. The short inflorescence, emanating from the leaf axils, is erect and carries three to six flowers with a diameter of 5–6 cm (2–$2\frac{1}{2}$ in). The wax-like flowers last for several weeks and are pleasantly scented. The tongue-shaped sepals and petals curve slightly forwards and are yellow to yellowish green. The petals are a little shorter and narrower than the 2.5–3 cm (1–$1\frac{1}{4}$ in) long sepals. The 3–3.5 cm ($1\frac{1}{4}$–$1\frac{3}{8}$ in) lip is fleshy and tri-lobed, coloured light yellow with red-brown stripes and spotting on the surface and is yellowish green underneath. The two small side lobes stand erect whereas the tongue-shaped central lobe, usually featuring two horns at its tip, hangs down a little. At the lip base is a sac-like continuation. The short, thick column is pale yellow.

Habitat Himalaya region (Nepal, Bhutan, Sikkim); at altitudes of approximately 1500 m

Flowering season Usually winter, spring. (5000 ft).

Vanda denisoniana

Characteristics This species, named after Lady Denison, has a short, stunted stem, covered with dense foliage and with long aerial roots. The leathery, strap-shaped leaves, having two teeth at their apices, reach a length of 20–30 cm (8–12 in) and a width of about 2 cm ($\frac{3}{4}$ in). The inflorescence is up to 15 cm (6 in) long and stands horizontally or slightly arched, carrying four to eight flowers loosely arranged. The wax-like, pleasantly scented and long-lasting flowers, about 5 cm (2 in) in size, have a pure white to greenish colour except for an orange patch at the base of the lip. The variety *V. denisoniana var. hebraica* Rchb.f. has flowers of a sulphur yellow with brownish markings, rather resembling Hebrew lettering (= *hebraica*). The sepals and petals are elliptically shaped developing towards the base into a short, broad bridge; they are sometimes slightly recurved. The lateral sepals are a little larger than the petals and the dorsal sepal. The lip is comparatively rather longer and consists of small erect side lobes of distorted oval shape and the violin-shaped central lobe which ends in two sections and carries four to five longitudinal keels. The spur is compressed at the sides and grows to no

Vanda cristata (× 1.2)

Vanda denisoniana (× 1.3)

more than 0.5 cm ($\frac{1}{8}$ in).
Habitat Burma (Arakan mountains); at altitudes
of 700–800 m (2300–2630 ft).
Flowering season Usually spring.

III Appendices

Appendix 1: Taxonomic chart of family Orchidaceae *

Plant families are divided by botanists into progressively more similar groups: those most commonly used are family, sub-family, tribe, sub-tribe, genus, species, often with a distinct suffix e.g. . . .oideae (subfamily), . . .eae (tribe), . . .inae (subtribe).

Sub-families

Apostasioideae †	**Cypripedioideae**	**Neottioideae**	**Orchidoideae**	**Epidendroideae**
Tribe **Apostasieae**	*Tribe* **Cypripedieae**	*Tribe* **Neottieae**	*Tribe* **Orchideae**	(See opposite page)
Genera Apostasia Adactylus Neuwiedia	*Genera* Cypripedium Paphiopedilum Phragmipedium Selenipedium	*Sub-tribe* **Limodorinae**	*Sub-tribe* **Epipogiinae**	
		Genera Cephalanthera Epipactis Limodorum	*Genera* Epipogium Stereosandra	
		Sub-tribe **Chloraeinae**	*Sub-tribe* **Orchidinae**	
		Genera Caladenia Chloraea	*Genera* Bonatea Galeorchis Habenaria Ophrys Platanthera Orchis Dactylorhiza Serapias Stenoglottis	
		Sub-tribe **Rhizanthellinae**		
		Genera Cryptanthemis Rhizanthella		
		Sub-tribe **Pterostylidinae**	*Sub-tribe* **Disinae**	
		Genera Caleana Pterostylis	*Genera* Disa Satyrium	
		Sub-tribe **Neottiinae**	*Sub-tribe* **Coryciinae**	
		Genera Listera Neottia	*Genera* Ceratandra Corycium	

---

* The scheme of classification shown in this chart is a further development of that used in the main text.
† A tiny group of very unorchidlike plants from the rain forests of Asia; possibly the primitive forerunners of typical orchids.

Sub-family Epidendroideae

Tribe
Gastrodieae
Sub-tribe
Vanillinae
Genera
Epistephium
Galeola
Vanilla
Sub-tribe
Gastrodiinae
Genera
Didymoplexis
Gastrodia

Sub-tribe
Poginiinae
Genera
Cleistes
Isotria
Nervilia
Pogonia
Triphora

Tribe
Epidendreae

Sub-tribe
Sobraliinae
Genera
Elleanthus
Isochilus
Palmorchis
Sobralia

Sub-tribe
Thuniinae
Genera
Arundina
Thunia

Sub-tribe
Arethusinae
Genus
Arethusa

Sub-tribe
Bletiinae
Genera
Acanthephippium
Bletia
Bletilla
Bothriochilus
Calanthe

Calopogon
Chysis
Coelia
Phaius
Sphathoglottis

Sub-tribe
Collabiinae
Genera
Chrysoglossum
Collabium
Nephelaphyllum
Tainia

Sub-tribe
Coelogyninae
Genera
Coelogyne
Dendrochilum
Panisea
Pholidota
Pleione

Sub-tribe
Epidendrinae
Genera
Barkeria
Brassavola
Broughtonia
Cattleya
Encyclia
Epidendrum
Hexisea
Laelia
Schomburgkia
Sophronitis

Sub-tribe
Eriinae
Genera
Appendicula
Eria
Gomera
Neobenthamia
Podochilus
Polystachya

Sub-tribe
Pleurothallidinae
Genera
Lepanthes
Masdevallia
Dracula

Pleurothallis
Restrepia
Stelis

Sub-tribe
Adrorhizinae
Genera
Adrorhizon
Josephia

Sub-tribe
Thelasiinae
Genera
Phreatia
Thelasis

Sub-tribe
Ridleyellinae
Genus
Ridleyella

Tribe
Malaxideae

Sub-tribe
Malaxidinae
Genera
Liparis
Malaxis
Oberonia

Sub-tribe
Dendrobiinae
Genera
Bulbophyllum
Dendrobium

Sub-tribe
Genyorchidinae
Genera
Drymoda
Genyorchis
Ione

Sub-tribe
Thecostelinae
Genus
Thecostele

Tribe
Vandeae
Sub-tribe
Cymbidiinae
Genera
Ansellia

Aplectrum
Corallorhiza
Cymbidiella
Cymbidium
Cyrtopodium
Eulophia
Eulophiella
Galeandra
Govenia
Grammatophyllum
Tipularia

Sub-tribe
Catasetinae
Genera
Catasetum
Cycnoches
Mormodes

Sub-tribe
Vandinae
Genera
Aërides
Angraecum
Campylocentrum
Dendrophylax
Luisia
Phalaenopsis
Renanthera
Stauropsis
Taeniophyllum
Trichoglottis
Vanda

Sub-tribe
Maxillariinae

Genera
Cryptocentrum
Maxillaria
Trigonidium
Xylobium

Sub-tribe
Lycastinae
Genera
Anguloa
Bifrenaria
Lycaste
Sub-tribe
Zygopetalinae
Genera
Aganisia

Chondrorhyncha
Huntleya
Pescatorea
Warrea
Zygopetalum

Sub-tribe
Stanhopeinae
Genera
Acineta
Coryanthes
Houlettia
Gongora
Peristeria
Sievekingia
Stanhopea

Sub-tribe
Ornithocephalinae
Genera
Centropetalum
Dichaea
Ornithocephalus
Pachyphyllum
Telipogon
Trichoceros

Sub-tribe
Oncidiinae
Genera
Aspasia
Brassia
Cochlioda
Comparettia
Gomesa
Ionopsis
Lockhartia
Miltonia
Notylia
Odontoglossum
Oncidium
Rodriguezia
Trichocentrum
Trichopilia

Appendix 2: Intergeneric hybrids of Oncidiinae

Adaglossum	Ada × Odontoglossum
Adioda	Ada × Cochlioda
Aliceara	Brassia × Miltonia × Oncidium
Aspasium	Oncidium × Aspasia
Aspoglossum	Odontoglossum × Aspasia

Bakerara	Brassia × Miltonia × Oncidium × Odontoglossum
Barbosaara	Cochlioda × Gomesoa × Odontoglossum × Oncidium
Beallara	Brassia × Cochlioda × Miltonia × Odontoglossum
Bradeara	Comparettia × Gomesa × Rodriguezia
Brapasia	Brassia × Aspasia
Brassada	Brassia × Ada
Brassidium	Brassia × Oncidium
Brassochilus	Brassia × Leochilus
Brummittara	Rodriguezia × Comparettia × Odontoglossum
Burrageara	Miltonia × Cochlioda × Odontoglossum × Oncidium

Campbellara	Rodriguezia × Oncidium × Odontoglossum
Charlesworthara	Oncidium × Cochlioda
Colmanara	Miltonia × Odontoglossum × Oncidium
Crawshayara	Aspasia × Brassia × Miltonia × Oncidium

Degarmoara	Brassia × Miltonia × Odontoglossum

Forgetara	Aspasia × Brassia × Miltonia

Goodaleara	Brassia × Cochlioda × Miltonia × Odontoglossum × Oncidium ×

Ionettia	Ionopsis × Comparettia
Ionocidium	Ionopsis × Oncidium
Lagerara	Aspasia × Cochlioda × Odontoglossum
Leocidium	Leochilus × Oncidium
Lockochilus	Leochilus × Lockhartia

Maclellanara	Brassia × Odontoglossum × Oncidium
Macradesa	Macradenia × Gomesa
Milpasia	Aspasia × Miltonia
Milpilia	Miltonia × Trichopilia
Miltassia	Brassia × Miltonia
Miltonidium	Miltonia × Oncidium
Miltonioda	Miltonia × Cochlioda

Notylidium	Notylia × Oncidium
Odontioda	Cochlioda × Odontoglossum
Odontobrassia	Brassia × Odontoglossum
Odontocidium	Odontoglossum × Oncidium
Odontonia	Odontoglossum × Miltonia
Odontorettia	Odontoglossum × Comparettia
Oncidenia	Macradenia × Oncidium
Oncidesa	Oncidium × Gomesa
Oncidettia	Oncidium × Comparettia
Oncidioda	Oncidium × Cochlioda
Oncidpilia	Oncidium × Trichopilia
Ornithocidium	Oncidium × Ornithophora
Rodrassia	Brassia × Rodriguezia
Rodrettia	Comparettia × Rodriguezia
Rodrettiopsis	Comparettia × Ionopsis × Rodriguezia
Rodridenia	Macradenia × Rodriguezia
Rodriopsis	Ionopsis × Rodriguezia
Rodritonia	Rodriguezia × Miltonia
Rodriglossum	Odontoglossum × Rodriguezia
Rodricidium	Rodriguezia × Oncidium

Sanderara	Brassia × Cochlioda × Odontoglossum
Schafferara	Aspasia × Brassia × Miltonia × Cochlioda × Odontoglossum
Trichocidium	Trichocentrum × Oncidium
Vanalstyneara	Miltonia × Odontoglossum × Oncidium × Rodriguezia
Vuylstekeara	Cochlioda × Miltonia × Odontoglossum
Warneara	Comparettia × Oncidium × Rodriguezia
Wilsonara	Cochlioda × Odontoglossum × Oncidium
Withnerara	Aspasia × Miltonia × Odontoglossum × Oncidium

Appendix 3: Intergeneric hybrids of Vandinae and related sub-tribes[*]

Genera: Acampe, Aërangis, Aëranthes, Aërides, Angraecum, Chiloschista, Cleisocentron, Cyrtorchis, Diploprora, Doritis, Eurychone, Gastrochilus, Kingiella, Luisa, Neofinetia, Ornithochilus, Parasarcochilus, Pelatantheria, Phalaenopsis, Plectorrhiza, Pomatocalpa, Renanthera, Rhinerrhiza, Saccolabium, Sarcochilus, Stauropsis, Taeniophyllum, Thrixspermum, Trichoglottis, Vanda and Vandopsis.

Aëridachnis	Aërides × Arachnis
Aëridisia	Aërides × Luisia
Aëriditis	Aërides × Doritis
Aëridocentrum	Aërides × Ascocentrum
Aëridochilus	Aërides × Sarcochilus
Aëridofinetia	Aërides × Neofinetia
Aeridoglossum	Aërides × Ascoglossum
Aëridopsis	Aërides × Phaleaenopsis
Aëridovanda	Aërides × Vanda
Angraeorchis	Angraecum × Cyrtorchis
Angrangis	Aërangis × Angraecum
Angranthes	Aëranthes × Angraecum
Arachnoglossum	Arachnis × Ascoglossum
Arachnoglottis	Arachnis × Trichoglottis
Arachnopsis	Arachnis × Phalaenopsis
Arachnostylis	Arachnis × Rhynchostylis
Aranda	Arachnis × Vanda
Aranthera	Arachnis × Renanthera
Ascandopsis	Ascocentrum × Vandopsis
Ascocenda	Ascocentrum × Vanda
Ascofinetia	Ascocentrum × Neofinetia
Asconopsis	Ascocentrum × Phalaenopsis
Ascorachnis	Arachnis × Ascocentrum
Ascovandoritis	Ascocentrum × Vanda × Doritis

Beardara	Ascocentrum × Doritis × Phalaenopsis
Bokchoonara	Arachnis × Ascocentrum × Phalaenopsis × Vanda
Bovornara	Arachnis × Ascocentrum × Rhynchostylis × Vanda
Burkillara	Aërides × Arachnis × Vandopsis

Carterara	Aërides × Renanthera × Vandopsis
Chewara	Aerides × Renanthera × Rhynchostylis
Chilocentrum	Ascocentrum × Chiloschista
Christieara	Aërides × Ascocentrum × Vanda
Chuanyenara	Arachnis × Renanthera × Rhynchostylis
Cleisonopsis	Cleisocentron × Phalaenopsis

Debruyneara	Ascocentrum × Luisia × Vanda
Devereuxara	Ascocentrum × Phalaenopsis × Vanda
Diplonopsis	Diploprora × Phalaenopsis
Dorandopsis	Doritis × Vandopsis
Doricentrum	Ascocentrum × Doritis
Doriella	Doritis × Kingiella
Doriellaopsis	Doritis × Kingiella × Phalaenopsis
Dorifinetia	Doritis × Neofinetia
Doriglossum	Ascoglossum × Doritis
Doristylis	Doritis × Rhynchostylis
Doritaenopsis	Doritis × Phalaenopsis
Dorthera	Doritis × Renanthera

Eastonara	Ascocentrum × Gastrochilus × Vanda
Edeara	Arachnis × Phalaenopsis × Renanthera × Vandopsis
Ernestara	Phalaenopsis × Renanthera × Vandopsis
Eurynopsis	Eurychone × Phalaenopsis

[*] Aëridinae, Sarcanthinae, Podanginae, Angraecinae, Aerangidinae

Freedara	Ascoglossum × Renanthera × Vandopsis
Fujioara	Ascocentrum × Trichoglottis × Vanda

Gastisia	Gastrochilus × Luisia
Gastrochiloglottis	Gastrochilus × Trichoglottis
Gastrosarcochilus	Gastrochilus × Sarcochilus
Goffara	Luisa × Rhynchostylis × Vanda
Gotterara	Ascocentrum × Renanthera × Vandopsis

Hagerara	Doritis × Phalaenopsis × Vanda
Hanesara	Aërides × Arachnis × Neofinetia
Hausermannara	Doritis × Phalaenopsis × Vandopsis
Hawaiiara	Renanthera × Vanda × Vandopsis
Himoriara	Ascocentrum × Phalaenopsis × Rhynchostylis × Vanda
Holttumara	Arachnis × Renanthera × Vanda
Hueylihara	Neofinetia × Renanthera × Rhynchostylis
Hugofreedara	Ascocentrum × Doritis × Kingiella

Irvingara	Arachnis × Renanthera × Trichoglottis

Joannara	Renanthera × Rhynchostylis × Vanda

Kagawara	Ascocentrum × Renanthera × Vanda
Komkrisara	Ascocentrum × Renanthera × Rhynchostylis

Laycockara	Arachnis × Phalaenopsis × Vandopsis
Leeara	Arachnis × Vanda × Vandopsis
Lewisara	Aërides × Arachnis × Ascocentrum × Vanda
Limara	Arachnis × Renanthera × Vandopsis
Lowsonara	Aërides × Ascocentrum × Rhynchostylis
Luascotia	Ascocentrum × Luisia × Neofinetia
Luinetia	Luisia × Neofinetia
Luinopsis	Luisia × Phalaenopsis
Luisanda	Luisia × Vanda
Luivanetia	Luisia × Neofinetia × Vanda
Lutherara	Phalaenopsis × Renanthera × Rhynchostylis
Lymanara	Aërides × Arachnis × Renanthera

Maccoyara	Aërides × Vanda × Vandopsis
Moirara	Phalaenopsis × Renanthera × Vanda
Mokara	Arachnis × Ascocentrum × Vanda

Appendix 3 continued

Nakamotoara	Ascocentrum × Neofinetia × Vanda
Neostylis	Neofinetia × Rhynchostylis
Ngara	Arachnis × Ascoglossum × Renanthera
Nobleara	Aërides × Renanthera × Vanda
Nonaara	Aërides × Ascoglossum × Renanthera
Onoara	Ascocentrum × Renanthera × Vanda × Vandopsis
Opsisanda	Vanda × Vandopsis
Opsistylis	Rhynchostylis × Vandopsis
Pageara	Ascocentrum × Luisia × Rhynchostylis × Vanda
Pantaapara	Ascoglossum × Renanthera × Vanda
Parachilus	Sarcochilus × Parasarcochilus
Paulsenara	Aërides × Arachnis × Trichoglottis
Pelacentrum	Ascocentrum × Pelatantheria
Perreiraara	Aërides × Rhynchostylis × Vanda
Phalaërianda	Aërides × Phalaenopsis × Vanda
Phalandopsis	Phalaenopsis × Vandopsis
Phalanetia	Neofinetia × Phalaenopsis
Phaliella	Kingiella × Phalaenopsis
Plectochilus	Plectorrhiza × Sarcochilus
Pomatisia	Luisia × Pomatocalpa

Renades	Aërides × Renanthera
Renafinanda	Neofinetia × Renanthera × Vanda
Renaglottis	Renanthera × Trichoglottis
Renancentrum	Ascocentrum × Renanthera
Renanetia	Renanthera × Neofinetia
Renanopsis	Renanthera × Vandopsis
Renanstylis	Renanthera × Rhynchostylis
Renantanda	Renanthera × Vanda
Renanthoglossum	Ascoglossum × Renanthera
Renanthopsis	Phalaenopsis × Renanthera
Rhinochilus	Rhinerrhiza × Sarcochilus
Rhynchocentrum	Ascocentrum × Rhynchostylis
Rhynchonopsis	Phalaenopsis × Rhynchostylis
Rhynchorides	Aërides × Rhynchostylis
Rhynchovanda	Rynchostylis × Vanda
Rhyndoropsis	Doritis × Phalaenopsis × Rhynchostylis
Richardmizutaara	Ascocentrum × Phalaenopsis × Vandopsis
Ridleyara	Arachnis × Trichoglottis × Vanda
Robinara	Aërides × Ascocentrum × Renanthera × Vanda
Rosakirchara	Ascocentrum × Neofinetia × Renanttera
Roseara	Doritis × Kingiella × Phalaenopsis × Renanthera
Rumrillara	Ascocentrum × Neofinetia × Rhynchostylis

Sagarikara	Aërides × Arachnis × Rhynchostylis
Sappanara	Arachnis × Phalaenopsis × Renanthera
Sarcocentrum	Ascocentrum × Sarcochilus
Sarconopsis	Phalaenopsis × Sarcochilus
Sarcothera	Renanthera × Sarcochilus
Sarcovanda	Sarcochilus × Vanda
Saridestylis	Aërides × Rhynchostylis × Sarcanthus
Sartylis	Sarcochilus × Rhynchostylis
Shigeuraara	Ascocentrum × Ascoglossum × Renanthera × Vanda
Stamariaara	Phalaenopsis × Ascocentrum × Renanthera × Vanda

Teohara	Arachnis × Renanthera × Vanda × Vandopsis
Thesaëra	Aërangis × Aëranthes
Trevorara	Arachnis × Phalaenopsis × Vanda
Trichonopsis	Phalaenopsis × Trichoglottis
Trichopsis	Trichoglottis × Vandopsis
Trichovanda	Trichoglottis × Vanda

Vandachnis	Arachnis × Vandopsis
Vandaenopsis	Phalaenopsis × Vanda
Vandewegheara	Ascocentrum × Doritis × Phalaenopsis × Vanda
Vandofinetia	Vanda × Neofinetia
Vandofinides	Aërides × Neofinetia × Vanda
Vandopsides	Aërides × Vandopsis
Vandoritis	Doritis × Vanda
Vanglossum	Ascoglossum × Vanda
Vascostylis	Ascocentrum × Rhynchostylis × Vanda

Wilkinsara	Ascocentrum × Vanda × Vandopsis

Yapara	Phalaenopsis × Rhynchostylis × Vanda
Yoneoara	Renanthera × Rhynchostylis × Vanda
Yuofara	Arachnis × Ascocentrum × Renanthera × Vanda

Appendix 4: Intergeneric hybrids of Epidendrinae

Genera: Barkeria, Brassavola (including Rhyncholaelia), Brassavola (including Rhyncholaelia), Broughtonia, Cattleya, Cattleyopsis, Diacrium (including Caularthron), Domingoa, Epidendrum (including Encyclia), Hexadesmia, Isabelia, Laelia, Laeliopsis, Leptotes, Nageliella, Schomburgkia Sophronitis (including Sophronitella), and Tetramicra.

Allenara	Cattleya × Diacrium × Epidendrum × Laelia
Arizara	Cattleya × Domingoa × Epidendrum
Bardendrum	Barkeria × Epidendrum
Bishopara	Broughtonia × Cattleya × Sophronitis
Bloomara	Broughtonia × Laeliopsis × Tetramicra
Brassocattleya	Brassavola × Cattleya
Brassodiacrium	Brassavola × Diacrium
Brassoepidendrum	Brassavola × Epidendrum
Brassoepilaelia	Brassavola × Epidendrum × Laelia
Brassolaelia	Brassavola × Laelia
Brassolaeliocattleya	Brassavola × Cattleya × Laelia
Brassophronitis	Brassavola × Sophronitis
Brassotonia	Brassavola × Broughtonia
Brownara	Broughtonia × Cattleya × Diacrium
Casoara	Brassavola × Broughtonia × Laeliopsis
Cattleyopsisgoa	Cattleyopsis × Domingoa
Cattleyopsistonia	Broughtonia × Cattleyopsis
Cattleytonia	Broughtonia × Cattleya
Dekensara	Brassavola × Cattleya × Schomburgkia
Diabroughtonia	Broughtonia × Diacrium
Diacattleya	Cattleya × Diacrium
Dialaelia	Diacrium × Laelia
Dialaeliocattleya	Cattleya × Diacrium × Laelia
Dialaeliopsis	Diacrium × Laeliopsis
Dillonara	Epidendrum × Laelia × Schomburgkia
Domindesmia	Domingoa × Hexadesmia
Domliopsis	Domingoa × Laeliopsis
Dunnara	Broughtonia × Cattleyopsis × Domingoa
Epibrassonitis	Brassavola × Epidendrum × Sophronitis
Epicatonia	Broughtonia × Cattleya × Epidendrum
Epicattleya	Cattleya × Epidendrum
Epidella	Epidendrum × Nageliella
Epidiacrium	Diacrium × Epidendrum
Epigoa	Domingoa × Epidendrum
Epilaelia	Epidendrum × Laelia
Epilaeliocattleya	Cattleya × Epidendrum × Laelia
Epilaeliopsis	Epidendrum × Laeliopsis
Epiphronitis	Epidendrum × Sophronitis
Epitonia	Broughtonia × Epidendrum
Fergusonara	Brassavola × Cattleya × Laelia × Schomburgkia × Sophronitis
Fujiwarara	Brassavola × Cattleya × Laeliopsis
Gauntlettara	Broughtonia × Cattleyopsis × Laeliopsis
Hartara	Broughtonia × Laelia × Sophronitis
Hawkesara	Cattleya × Cattleyopsis × Epidendrum
Hawkinsara	Broughtonia × Cattleya × Laelia × Sophronitis
Herbertara	Cattleya × Laelia × Schomburgkia × Sophronitis
Hildaara	Broughtonia × Laeliopsis × Schomburgkia
Hookerara	Brassavola × Cattleya × Diacrium

Isanitella	Isabelia × Sophronitella
Iwanagara	Brassavola × Cattleya × Diacrium × Laelia
Izumiara	Cattleya × Epidendrum × Laelia × Schomburgkia × Sophronitis
Jimenezara	Broughtonia × Laelia × Laeliopsis
Kawamotoara	Brassavola × Cattleya × Domingoa × Epidendrum × Laelia
Kirchara	Cattleya × Epidendrum × Laelia × Sophronitis
Laeliocatonia	Broughtonia × Cattleya × Laelia
Laeliocattkeria	Barkeria × Cattleya × Laelia
Laeliokeria	Barkeria × Laelia
Laeliopleya	Cattleya × Laeliopsis
Laelonia	Broughtonia × Laelia
Lemaireara	Broughtonia × Cattleyopsis × Epidendrum
Leptolaelia	Laelia × Leptotes
Leptovola	Brassavola × Leptotes
Liaopsis	Laelia × Laeliopsis
Lioponia	Broughtonia × Laeliopsis
Lowara	Brassavola × Laelia × Sophronitis
Lyonara	Trichoglottis × Vanda
Macleanoreara	Brassavola × Laelia × Schomburgkia
Mizutara	Cattleya × Diacrium × Schomburgkia
Moscosoara	Broughtonia × Epidendrum × Laeliopsis
Nashara	Broughtonia × Cattleyopsis × Diacrium
Northenara	Cattleya × Epidendrum × Laelia × Schomburgkia

Osmentara	Broughtonia × Cattleya × Laeliopsis
Potinara	Brassavola × Cattleya × Laelia × Sophronitis
Recchara	Brassavola × Cattleya × Laelia × Schomburgkia
Rolfeara	Brassavola × Cattleya × Sophronitis
Rothara	Brassavola × Cattleya × Epidendrum × Laelia × Sophronitis
Schombavola	Brassavola × Schomburgkia
Schombocatonia	Broughtonia × Cattleya × Schomburgkia
Schombocattleya	Cattleya × Schomburgkia
Schombodiacrium	Diacrium × Schomburgkia
Schomboepidendrum	Epidendrum × Schomburgkia
Schombolaelia	Laelia × Schomburgkia
Schombonia	Broughtonia × Schomburgkia
Schombonitis	Schomburgkia × Sophronitis
Scullyara	Cattleya × Epidendrum × Schomburgkia
Shipmanara	Broughtonia × Diacrium × Schomburgkia
Sophrocattleya	Cattleya × Sophronitis
Sophrolaelia	Laelia × Sophronitis
Sophrolaeliocattleya	Cattleya × Laelia × Sophronitis
Stacyara	Cattleya × Epidendrum × Sophronitis
Stanfieldara	Epidendrum × Laelia × Sophronitis

Appendix 4 continued

Tetrakeria	Barkeria × Tetramicra
Tetraliopsis	Laeliopsis × Tetramicra
Tetratonia	Broughtonia × Tetramicra
Tuckerara	Cattleya × Diacrium × Epidendrum
Vaughnara	Brassavola × Cattleya × Epidendrum
Westara	Brassavola × Broughtonia × Cattleya × Laelia × Schomburgkia
Yahiroara	Brassavola × Cattleya × Epidendrum × Laelia × Schomburgkia
Yamadara	Brassavola × Cattleya × Epidendrum × Laelia

Appendix 5: Glossary

Aberrant Deviating from the normal type.

Abortive Arrested in development.

Abrupt Truncated; suddenly changing in shape and size.

Acaulescent Stemless.

Acicular Needle-like.

Acotyledonous Without cotyledons

Acropetal The order in which the parts of a plant arise; applied to flowers produced in succession from a common axis.

Aculeate Set with prickles.

Acuminate Tapering to a point.

Acute Terminating abruptly in a sharp point.

Adnate Adhering; united.

Adventitious Appearing casually or in unusual places.

Aerial Existing and growing in the air.

Aggregate Collected into one mass.

Alternate Alternatively placed occurring first on one side and then on the other of an axial line such as a stem; not opposite or paired.

Amplexicaul Leaves embracing the stem at their base.

Ancipitous Two-edged as in the pseudobulbs of *Oncidium* and others.

Annulate Marked with rings, as in the fleshy stems of *Phaius* and others.

Anterior The side to the front.

Anther The part of the stamen containing the pollen.

Anthesis Full flower.

Apetalous Without petals.

Apex The top, tip or pointed end.

Aphyllous Without leaves, naturally leafless.

Apiculate Having a minute apex.

Approximate Not joined but placed close together.

Arachnoid Spider-like.

Arcuate Bow-shaped.

Articulate Jointed.

Ascending Growing upwards.

Asexual Sexless.

Attenuate Long, narrow and tapering.

Axil Upper angle formed with the stem by a leaf or branch.

Axile Referring to the axis.

Barbate Bearded.

Bibracteate Having two opposite bracts, one usually larger than the other, as in Paphiopedilums *callosum* and *niveum*.

Bifid Separated into two equal parts.

Bifoliate Two-leaved.

Bigeneric Hybrids having two genera in their pedigree.

Blade Expanded part of a leaf or petal.

Bracheate Parts at right angles and arranged alternately.

Bract A small leaf-like member below a flower.

Bulbose Inflated at the base; with a bulb.

Caespitose or Cespitose Growing in thick tufts or clumps.

Calcarate Spurred.

Calceolate; Calciform Slipper-shaped.

Calli Plural of callus.

Callosity Part which is thickened and hardened.

Callus A hard protuberance.

Campanulate Bell-shaped.

Canaliculate Grooved longitudinally; channelled.

Capitate Having the inflorescence in a head.

Capsule The seed vessel.

Carinate Keeled.

Carnose Fleshy.

Cauda A tail.

Caudicle Small stalk of the pollinia.

Cauline Of or belonging to the stem.

Ciliate Fringed with hairs.

Clavate Club-shaped.

Cleistogamous Fertilization within the unopened flower.

Clinandrium The chamber at the top of the column housing the pollinia.

Clone Members of a population of plants derived by vegetative propagation from one original plant.

Coherent Joined together.

Column The upright structure formed by the union of the stamens with the style. The gymnostemium.

Complicate Part of the leaves being folded.

Compressed Flattened.
Conduplicate The leaves being folded lengthwise along the middle.
Congested Crowded very closely.
Connate In orchids, applied to two similar organs that grow together along their sides.
Connivent Converging.
Convolute Rolled up, the edges overlapping.
Cordate Heart-shaped.
Corymbose A modification of the raceme in which the flower-stalks are progressively shorter towards the apex.
Costate Ribbed.
Cotyledon The seed-leaf.
Crenate Having the edge scalloped.
Crenulate Finely scalloped.
Crest A raised ridge, usually on the lip of some orchids.
Cristate In the form of a crest.
Cucullate Hooded.
Cuneate Wedge-shaped, tapering towards the base.
Cupular Cup-shaped.
Cymbiform Boat-shaped.
Cytology The study of cells and their formation.

Damping-down Used by glass-house growers; meaning to damp the paths, walls and benches, but not the compost in which the plants have been potted.
Decurrent Extending downwards.
Dehiscent Splitting of a ripe fruit to discharge its seed.
Deltoid Triangular.
Denticulate Having small teeth at the margin.
Dialysis Two like organs normally joined together becoming separate. The opposite of *Connate*.
Dichotomous Branching in pairs.
Dicotyledon A flowering plant having two cotyledons or seed lobes.
Digitate Finger-like parts radiating from one side only, from a common centre.
Diphyllous Stems and pseudobulbs producing two leaves at their apices.
Distichous Two rows on opposite sides of the stem.
Diurnal Daily.
Dolabriform Axe-shaped.

Ecology The branch of biology dealing with, collectively, the mutual relations between organisms and their environment.
Ellipsoid A solid of which all the plane sections through one of the axes are ellipses and all the other sections ellipses or circles.
Elliptical Oval narrowed to rounded ends.

Elongated In botany, long in proportion to its breadth.
Emarginate A leaf, foliage or floral, having a shallow notch at the apex.
Ensiform Straight, narrow and with the point acute; sword-shaped.
Epiphyte A plant which grows on another plant, but which does not draw nourishment from it.
Equitant Leaves folded one over the other at their bases.

Falcate Sickle-shaped.
Filiform Thread-like.
Fimbriate Finely fringed margin.
Foleaceous Leaf-like in appearance and texture.
Fusiform Spindle-shaped.

Galeate Helmet-shaped.
Genetics The part of biology dealing with heredity and variation.
Glabrous Smooth and hairless.
Glaucous Covered with a bloom, whitish, greenish or bluish.
Gregarious Growing in clusters.
Gymnostemium Column.

Hastate Halberd-shaped.
Hispid Covered with stiff, short hairs.

Imbricating Overlapping like roof tiles.
Internode Part of the stem between the nodes or joints.
Involute When the lateral margins of a sepal, petal etc., are rolled inwards towards the blade.
Isthmus The narrowed portion of a part of a flower.

Keel A projecting ridge on a surface.

Lamina The flat, extended part of a floral segment, or leaf; the blade.
Lanceolate Lance-shaped, broadest in the middle.
Lateral The side of an organ.
Lead In epiphytes, a new growth, partly matured, which will become the new pseudobulb.
Liguiform Tongue-shaped.
Ligulate Strap-shaped.
Linnear Narrow, with the edges parallel.
Lithophyte A plant living on stone or rock.
Lobe A rounded projection of part of a leaf or other organ.

Maculate Spotted.
Median The mid-rib of a symmetrical leaf.
Micropyle The minute opening in the ovule through which the pollen enters.
Monandrous With one stamen.

Monocotyledon With a single seed leaf.
Monoecious With male and female flowers on the same plant but in separate inflorescences.
Monophyllous Pseudobulbs and stems producing one leaf at their apices.
Monopodial Growth from the apex only. Opposite of sympodial.
Morphology The branch of biology dealing with the form of animals and plants and the various influences which affect that form.
Multigeneric Including several or many genera.

Nodule A small node or knot in the stem or other part of the plant.
Node A joint on the stem from which the leaves spring.
Nomenclature The system of naming.

Obcordate Narrow at the base and terminating with two rounded lobes; the opposite of cordate.
Oblanceolate When the blade is broader between the middle and the apex. The opposite of lanceolate.
Oblong The sides parallel and nearly straight, two or three times as long as broad.
Orbicular Spherical.
Orographic The functions and features of mountains.
Ovate Egg-shaped in outline.
Ovoid Egg-shaped three-dimensionally.

Panduriform Fiddle-shaped.
Paniculate A branching inflorescence.
Parasite An organism living on another (the host), and drawing its nourishment directly from it.
Parthenogenesis Reproduction without involving sex, asexually.
Pathology Study of the causes and cures of diseases.
Pectinate Like the teeth of a comb.
Pedicel The lateral or secondary flower stalk of a raceme or panicle.
Peduncle The flower stalk.
Pendulous Hanging.
Perianth The series of floral segments surrounding the sexual organs. The calyx and the corolla. In orchids it is sometimes restricted to the lower whorl or sepals.
Petiolate Leaves having a footstalk.
Petiole The footstalk of a leaf.
Pistil The female organ of a flower; the ovary, style and stigma.
Plicate Fan-shaped or folded.
Pollen The male element produced by the anther.
Pollinia The masses of pollen in the anther.
Posterior At the back.
Primordia Earliest formed in the course of growth, leaves, fruit, etc.; applied to tissues in their rudimentary stage.

Pubescent Hairy.
Pyriform Pear-shaped.

Raceme Inflorescence where the flowers are arranged on pedicels along an undivided axis.
Rachis The axis or stem of an inflorescence.
Recurved Bent back.
Reniform Kidney-shaped.
Resupinated Turned back or twisted upwards.
Revolute Rolled backwards under the blade. Opposite of involute.

Saccate Having a bag-like depression.
Saggitate Like an arrow head.
Scandent Climbing by attachment to neighbouring bodies.
Scape In orchids, the peduncles that grow from the base of pseudobulbs.
Scarious Dry and membranous.
Serrate Like the teeth of a saw.
Sessile Stalkless.
Sinuate The margin being alternately convex and concave.
Spathulate Spoon-shaped; narrow at the base and broader and rounded at the apex.
Species A group or class of plants (usually a sub-division of a genus) having certain and permanent characteristics which distinguish it from other groups within the genus.
Spermatophyte A seed-producing plant.
Spike Scape.
Spur A tubular expansion, resembling a cock's spur in form, of a sepal or petal, usually producing nectar.
Stamen The male organ of a flower in two parts – the anther containing the pollen and the filament, a slender stalk supporting the anther.
Staminode An abortive stamen or organ resembling it, without an anther.
Stellate Like a star's rays.
Stigma That part of the pistil which receives the pollen in impregnation and which, in orchids, is sited on the under side of the top of the column.
Stipule A lateral appendage (often resembling a small leaf or scale) borne in pairs upon the leaf-base of certain plants.
Striate Striped.
Subgenus A taxonomic division of a large genus.
Subulate Awl-shaped, cylindrical.
Sympodial Axial growth continued by lateral shoots; opposite of monopodial.

Taxonomy That department of science which relates to classification.
Terete Cylindrical.

Terrestrial Of the earth; growing in the soil.

Tessellated Having a pattern forming a mosaic; chequered or marbled.

Tomentose Covered with short matted hairs.

Trapeziform Like a trapeze. An irregular quadrilateral.

Tribe A group forming a division of an order and containing a number of genera.

Tridentate Terminating in three teeth.

Trigonal Three-angled.

Triquetral Three-edged.

Truncate Cut off abruptly.

Tuberous An underground rhizome.

Umbel Inflorescence in which the pedicels grow from the same point in the peduncle and diverge like the ribs of an umbrella.

Unguiculate The blade of a floral segment narrowed at the base into a short petiole or claw.

Variety A division of a species differing from the species in some minor but permanent and transmissible particular; also much used to describe hybrids.

Vector A carrier of disease.

Ventral Belonging to the anterior or lower surface as in the ventral sepal of a paphiopedilum.

Vestigial Remaining or surviving in a degenerate, atrophied or inferior condition or form.

Viscid; viscous Sticky.

Whorl Three or more members, foliaceous or floral, in a circle about an axis.

Xerophyte A plant adapted to survive on a limited supply of moisture.

Zygomorphic Symmetrical about a single plane, divisible into similar lateral halves in one way only.

Index

Page numbers in bold type designate
colour photographs